A Manual of Calligraphy

· Dedication ·

This book owes much to many but especially to my
parents who for many years suffered my submergence
in the craft, and to my wife Heather for also bearing the anti-
social hours and preparation.

It is also dedicated to Barbara Nichol, whose book this could
have been, and those who have passed on their knowledge so
freely to me, particularly Michael Gullick, Donald Jackson,
Kennedy Smith and those scribes and students whose ideas
have influenced my own.

A Manual of
of
Calligraphy

Peter E. Taylor

UNWIN HYMAN

London Sydney Wellington

First published in Great Britain 1988
This book is copyright under the Berne Convention.
No reproduction without permission. All rights reserved.

Unwin Hyman. A Division of Unwin Hyman Ltd.,
40 Museum Street, London WC1A 1LU, UK.

Unwin Hyman. A Division of Unwin Hyman Ltd.,
Park Lane, Hemel Hempstead, Herts HP2 4TE, UK.

Allen & Unwin Australia Pty. Ltd.,
8 Napier Street, North Sydney, NSW 2060, Australia.

Allen & Unwin with the Port Nicholson Press
PO Box 11838, Wellington, New Zealand.

© Peter E. Taylor 1988

Devised and produced by
Taylor-Type Publications (Australia) Pty. Ltd.

British Library Cataloguing in Publication Data

Taylor, Peter E.
A Manual of Calligraphy
    1. Calligraphy
    1. Title
745·61 X43
ISBN 0-04-44-0125-6

Designed by Richard Pieremont

Printed by Dah Hua, Hong Kong

·Contents·

· Introduction ·

A calligrapher's enjoyment does not come solely from achievement of a completed piece of beautiful writing. It also comes from the experience of personal expression in the lovely flow of letter shapes, much as the dancer projects himself in the rhythm and pattern of the dance. He carefully selects styles of script, flourishes, colour and techniques from his repertoire, to enable him to design and create a very personal response to the text, or to use letters and words as elements of pattern and design in themselves

The aim of this book is to enable the beginner to design and enjoy creating beautiful writing, based on the sound principles of the specifications of letters perfected over the centuries. It is also hoped that it will serve both beginners and those with experience by increasing their awareness of the possibilities of each script and that the examples and techniques described for illumination, colour, and design will act as a stimulus for the personal development of all calligraphers.

1· ·A·Short·History·of·Writing·

It is hard to imagine a world without writing. Even our earliest ancestors must have needed to record matters such as ownership of property or where the best hunting grounds were. Today we can still see their cave paintings and the small pictures we call hieroglyphics. It must have been a very slow procedure for the Egyptians to carve so much of their hieroglyphic writing into stone. In Babylonia it was discovered that marks made in clay could be baked for a permanent record. For the Romans, wax tablets allowed marks to be made quickly. These were sealed in wooden boxes for privacy and later destroyed by rubbing the surface.

Perhaps the biggest revolution in the history of writing was the series of inventions which enabled writing to be easily transported. The first 'paper' was probably made from strips of papyrus, a sedge. Thin lengths of pithy material were laid across each other at right angles and beaten with a stone or piece of wood to remove the air and liberate the juice which, when the strips were placed under pressure, helped them to stick together. Frayed ends from chewed rush stems produced a brush, and ink was carbon, with a gum to stop the carbon flaking off when dry.

It was so much quicker for Egyptian scribes to write on papyrus, that they took short cuts in drawing their hieroglyphics, which became simplified. Whereas, initially, a picture of an owl stood simply for an owl, it became the symbol of an idea – wisdom. Simple pictures eventually stood only for sounds – the word for ox started with an 'A' sound, and further changes were made with the mixing of cultures. When the Phoenicians reached Greece the ox picture was incorporated with their 'alpha' to become A. In Rome it was carved in stone to give our capital A.

Egyptian

On papyrus

Phoenician

Greek

Roman

Our western alphabet, though with an Arabic foundation, is based particularly on Classical Roman letters. The stone to be written on was probably divided into squares and the letters painted before they were cut, using a hammer & chisel.

The serifs on the corners of letters arose because it is very difficult to cut square corners into stone. They give the letters elegance, & make them easier to read over a distance. The Romans used papyrus from Egypt for scrolls, and wax tablets, which they marked with a stylus, for everyday work.

When beautiful writing was needed on papyrus or vellum (calf or goat skin) in the production of books, for example, scribes tried to copy the thick and thin lines of the capitals carved into stone. To achieve this the reed & quill were cut to make

FiFTH CENTVRY ROMAN CAPITALS

a square-ended or 'edged' pen. The thick and thin marks could then be easily produced by direction of pen movement only. Square capitals similar to those drawn above may have been reserved for the most important manuscripts. The faster written rustic capitals were used for most books, though both styles were in use until about the fifth century.

RVSTIC CAPITALS

PATER NOSTER QVI ES IN COELIS SANCTIFICETVR NOMEN TVVM

By the fourth century Roman Uncial letters had been developed. These, too, were essentially capitals and were used for the finest books until about the eighth century. As greater writing speed became necessary, so the shapes were again changed, producing what we now call minuscule, or small letters. Many of these were first formalised in the seventh century, and from then onwards such minuscules have been used for most lengthy works. Although slight variations occurred, these styles were used in all countries under Roman rule.

ROMAN
UNCIAL FIFTH CENTURY
and half uncial
MUCH EARLY
UNCIAL WRITING
WAS THIS SIZE OR SMALLER

With the collapse of the Roman Empire writing almost died out. It was kept alive by monks in inaccessible areas of the former Empire, where it was made as beautiful as possible, and elaborate decoration was added. The Irish Half-uncial is seen at its best in the Book of Kells, written in the eighth century. English Half-uncials were modelled on the Irish pattern.

Whilst English and Irish writing was based on the Roman Uncial, in Europe styles derived more from Roman cursive or 'everyday' script.

It was during the reign of Charlemagne that writing activity increased. Under his patronage, at the monastery of St Martin in Tours, under Abbot Alcuin of York, classical Greek and Roman manuscripts were copied and church books revised and rewritten. The style used was the Caroline, or Carolingian hand, which the scribes formalised for their task. The earliest version is in the Bible written for Maurdramnus, who died in 778. The precision of the script was developed during Alcuin's rule at Tours from 796 to 804, and it is important because of the influence of the caroline Minuscule in the shaping of our present-day alphabet.

carolingian minuscule

The use of the Caroline Minuscule spread throughout Europe. By the tenth century a variation was being used in southern England, though the characteristic roundness and angle of the thinnest marks to the writing line was retained. The style gave flexibility for compression, and therefore economy on time, affecting the size and cost of books. By the thirteenth and fourteenth centuries, compression had occurred to such an extent that much use was made of small writing consisting mainly of vertical thick strokes with almost touching angled apices. This Gothic writing gave a very solid appearance to the piece of work, but it is now considered difficult to read quickly.

In Italy, in both architecture and letter forms, the Gothic angularity was never carried to the same extreme as in northern Europe, and with further study of the rounded eleventh and twelfth century Carolingian hands a related Humanistic style was developed during the Renaissance. The shapes which evolved became a basis for writing and typefaces and, although Gothic faces were used in Germany up until this century, over the last 400 years it has been the Roman typeface that has been the most popular.

Mr. P. Bull,
1, Ide Street,
S·T·A·F·F·O·R·D,
9.4053.

Italic writing was also developed in Italy during the Renaissance, enabling greater speed to be used for it has an easy flowing rhythm, is compressed, has joins between many letters and a reduction of serifs. It is still much used for type, manuscripts and handwriting.

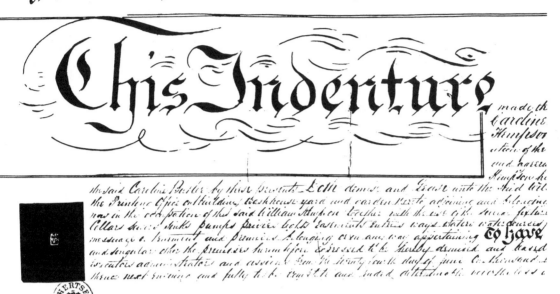

Though Copperplate writing developed as an imitation of that engraved for printing, with the increased use of printing most skills of the scribe were lost until the end of the nineteenth century. For example, as shown above, Victorian attempts at a gothic script consisted of drawing outlines of letters and infilling with a brush or many pen strokes.

The arts and crafts revival, stimulated by John Ruskin & William Morris, provided the atmosphere in which Edward Johnston began his study of manuscripts in the British Museum in 1897; their materials, and the tools and techniques of their production. When we study a script today we take for granted that we look for the relationship between nib width and letter height, the angle between the writing line and the thinnest nib line, and the space between

lines of writing. It is hard for us to realise that such funda-
mentals had to be rediscovered. When Johnston started
teaching he stimulated all who attended to strive for ex-
cellence, and demand for instruction soon exceeded facilit-
ies. In 1906 his book 'Writing and Illuminating and Lettering'
was published. Today, it is still popular and being reprinted.
It is largely due to Johnston that calligraphy has flourished
this century, and continues to do so.

The popularity and uses of calligraphy have increased year
by year. New styles of alphabet are continually developing, &
each calligrapher puts his own character even on the standard
formal scripts, and has his own ideas on beauty of arrange-
ment and decoration.

The remainder of this book is devoted to learning the craft
~ hopefully enabling the student to become competent in, and
enjoy, writing several styles. However, works of art will only
be produced when practice has produced confidence in personal craftsmanship. This leads to that magical fluidity
or freedom which is one hallmark of the best calligraphy.

2· ·ROMAN· ·CAPITALS·

The Roman capital letters drawn and described here are for study rather than immediate copying. These shapes have provided the foundation for all western scripts developed over the centuries. The notes provide an insight into the sort of properties to look for, and measurements to make, to determine the proportions of any style being studied.

The inscription honouring Emperor Trajan on the Trajan column (circa A.D.114) in Rome is considered to provide the supreme example of capital letters. By learning more about the basic structure of each letter, it is hoped that their important proportions will be recognised and reproduced in other scripts. When personal alphabets are designed, though the character of letters may be changed through different emphasis, beauty & legibility are maintained through use of sound foundations. No part will then be over-exaggerated or dwarfed.

Most of the Roman alphabet was based directly on that of the Greeks, with many letters unchanged, some revised, & new ones added. H, J, K, U, W, Y and Z are not present on the Trajan inscription. H was contained in the Roman alphabet at this

17

time, but the others have been added later. The examples drawn here have been designed using the same principles of construction as the original letters. How the letters were marked and carved into stone is still a matter of conjecture – especially the formation of the serifs, but it is thought that the stone was marked out in squares and the letters painted with a brush first.

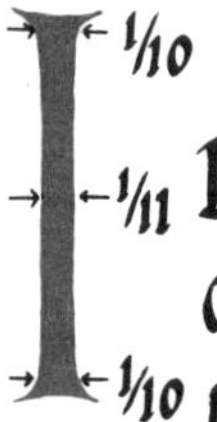

I ← $\frac{1}{10}$ The proportions of the letter I are used in the verticals of
→ ← $\frac{1}{11}$ B, D, E, F, H, J, K, L, P, R, T and U. The sides are slightly con-
cave, $\frac{1}{10}$th of the letter height at the extremities, $\frac{1}{11}$th at
← $\frac{1}{10}$ the centre line. O is only fractionally
narrower than a perfect circle, and the outside is symmetrical about the vertical axis.
The internal ellipse is tilted to the left. It overlaps the guide lines fractionally.

   As most of the alphabet letters contain an element of the
letter I or O, the structure of these two control the design of the
other letters.

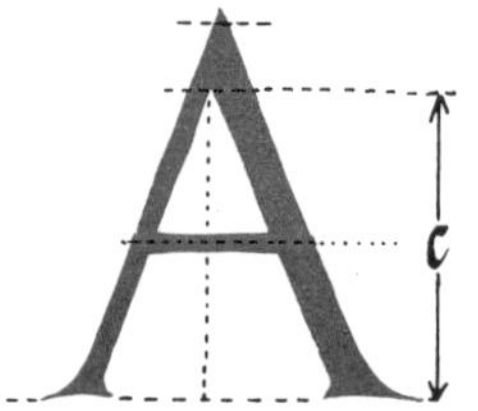

A   The width of letter A is a little more than $\frac{5}{6}$ths
of the height. The wide stroke is $\frac{1}{10}$th of the
letter height, the left hand stroke $\frac{2}{3}$ of a wide
stroke and the cross stroke half of the wide stroke (midway between the inside of the top angle
and the base line). The outside of the top angle overlaps the
guide line by about a $\frac{1}{4}$ of a wide stroke. The inner serifs are
the smallest.

18

The basic structure of B is two D's on top of each other, the internal areas being approximately in the ratio of 5:6. The thinnest parts are shown by arrows, and the thickest by dots, derived from the outer circles and inner tilted ellipses. The vertical has the proportions of 1, though note that the inner angle is sharp at the top, and the lower angle is curved. upper and lower horizontals overlap the guide lines, and are less than half the thickness of a wide stroke.

The outside curve of the letter C is part of an almost perfect circle. Like the letter O the inner curve is tilted to the left. The upper serif is heavier than the lower one. Their outer extremities can be connected by a vertical line. The top arm is flatter than the lower arm in relation to the horizontal. Both upper and lower extremities of the letter overlap the guide lines.

The outside curve of D is almost circular. The thin parts are less than ½ of a wide stroke. Like other round letters, the upper and lower extremities extend above and below the writing line. From the vertical, the top arm ascends slightly, and the lower descends. Internally, the join with the vertical is angular at the top, whilst the lower limb grows from the vertical, so forming a curve.

Both E and F are approximately half a square in shape, though the upper arm of the F may be fractionally longer than that of E. A vertical line can connect upper and lower serifs of the E, as shown, but whereas the middle arm of E rests on the centre line, the lower stroke of the F is bisected by it. The horizontals are about half as wide as the wide stroke. The horizontal of L is the same size and shape as the lower limb of E, an ogee curve.

The structure of G is much the same as that of C. The vertical comes almost to the centre line and usually is best drawn at an angle to the lower arm, rather than blending with it. In the letter H the proportion of width to height is about 7:8. The horizontal is half the width of the verticals, and rests on the centre line.

The width of K at the top is about 2/3rds the width of the base. Height and base are almost equal. The vertical and lower diagonals are of equal width, with the upper diagonal half this width. On diagonal strokes of any letter serifs are drawn out in the direction of the stroke, being kept smaller on the inside.

J was not specialised as a letter until the 15th century. It has the same structure as I with a curved extension.

20

M

The verticals of M splay slightly to increase the internal angles a little. The first and third strokes are ⅔rds of the width of the second & fourth wide strokes. Upper points project above the guideline by ¼ of a wide stroke, and both diagonals of the V curve inwards towards the base.

N

The proportion of width to height in the letter N is 7:8. Verticals are 3/4 of the wide diagonal stroke, which curves towards the base. The left apex extends above the guideline.

Q P

Q is similar to O except for the tail.

P fits into half a square. The top limb ascends from the vertical forming an internal angle. The outside curve is quite circular, projecting fractionally above the guideline, and terminating half a wide stroke below the centre line. The bowl of R is deeper than that of P, joining the vertical the width of a wide stroke below the centre line. The bowl straightens to allow the tail to join almost at right angles. As with K the tail may be curved or end with a serif at its tip.

R

S

In common with C, the top arm of letter S is flattened at the top, but the inner curve is maintained to form the serif. This is vertically in line with the outside of the lower curve. With the lower internal area being slightly larger than the upper one, the letter appears to tilt a little forward. Note the serif angles.

The width of letter T is approximately $\frac{7}{9}$ths of its height, with the horizontal $\frac{2}{3}$rds the width of the vertical. Slightly more weight may be given to the left arm when the letter is terminal, and less weight to the right side. The crossbar tilts slightly down to the right side. Note also that the angle of the left serif is greater than that on the right hand side.

The thinnest part of U is not on the baseline, owing to the tilted inner ellipse. This means that the curved part of the letter U meets the vertical almost with a point. The width to height ratio is 7:8. The serif at the base of the vertical only projects to the right, and may be tilted upwards a little.

SQVE·ROMAN

Part of the Trajan Column

NERVAE·F·NER

V is slightly wider than A, with both strokes curving towards the base to make a point on the line. (Oblique strokes of A are straight.) The first stroke is the width of a normal wide stroke, & the second stroke 2/3rds of this. W is made up of two V's, with the lowest part of the crossing sitting on the centre line.

X is approximately 7/9ths of its height in width. The narrow stroke is half of the wide one

The width to height ratio is 7:8 in the letter Y. The narrow stroke is half that of a wide one.

The width to height ratio of Z is 3/4. The upper horizontal and lower limb are not entirely parallel. The lower arm has a fractional downward tilt. The top of the diagonal curves in slightly, & and the upper serif angles inwards.

3· ·Tools·for·the·Job

As with many hobbies, calligraphy costs little to make a start. As one progresses, however, one tends to experiment with different types of pens, inks and papers. This may add to the expense of the hobby, but it is useful to build one's confidence in mastering a wide range of media.

All calligraphic styles require a broad-edged, chisel-shaped nib, with the exception of Copperplate, where thick and thin lines are produced by pressure changes on a pointed, flexible nib. Most beginners start with a calligraphy pen set, which consists of a fountain pen and a number of interchangeable nibs. Some fountain pens use cartridges, some fill only with 'squeeze fillers', others still may use both. For some fountain pens, there are many varieties of extra nibs available. There is no particular pen which is superior to others. One should simply weigh up comfort, characteristics, price and usefulness. For example, there is no point in buying 1 cm (1/2 in) wide nibs if one only wants to develop elegant handwriting.

An alternative to the fountain pen is to cut one's own quill, bamboo or reed pen. Bamboo pens, and those made from reeds, work very well on paper, because both the implement & writing surface are of vegetable origin. By the same token, quills are beautiful to use on vellum, which is made from animal skin (goat, calf or kangaroo). Details of their construction and use will be found in chapter 16. One of their advantages is that they can be cut to suit the individual's most comfortable writing position, as shown below.

Another alternative to the fountain pen is the dip nib. These nibs are capable of producing very fine lines and are easier to use with colour, but overall are not as convenient as fountain pens. Most calligraphers use them (or quills) for the final execution of a commission, restricting the fountain pen to 'rough copies' or casual writing. Brause nibs and William Mitchell's Roundhand nibs are used for most small writing. William Mitchell's nibs range from sizes 00 to 6, but 1½ to 3½ are the most useful to start with. They all fit into a standard pen holder. Sizes

Dip nibs :—
1. Speedball Steel-Brush · 2. Coit · 3. Automatic ·
4. Speedball C Series · 5. William Mitchell's · 6. Brause ·

smaller than 3½ are difficult to use, because slight changes in pressure cause comparatively large changes in line thickness of letters. For larger writing, Speedball nibs size c2–c0 are very useful, and for large or decorative pieces Speedball Steel Brushes, Coit or 'Automatic' pens are invaluable.

Brause and Speedball c series nibs are already equipped with a reservoir to retain ink. William Mitchell's nibs, however, require one to be fitted. It slides over the underside of the nib so that it just touches the metal of the nib. It is important that it must touch, but not part, the nib so time should be spent taking the reservoir on and off and bending it until it fits correctly.

One should pull the reservoir back from the tip of the nib so that the distance from the nib tip to the reservoir tip is not less than 2mm (¹⁄₁₆in) for small sizes, and about the same distance back as the nib is wide for larger ones.

New nibs have a layer of grease on them to prevent rust, and this may need to be removed before the ink is able to flow easily. Dipping them into methylated spirit, boiling water or using saliva are all suitable treatments. Passing the nib through a flame tends to detemper the metal.

No nib should be overfilled. The amount shown here is ideal. It is usually convenient to place ink in a bottle top, so that the nib cannot be dipped in too far. The nib should then be wiped on a piece of paper, suede or sponge and tested to make sure that it is producing fine thin lines, before continuing to write on the piece of work in progress.

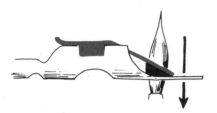

One can also fill nibs with a dropper, or brush ink or thin paint on the side of the nib. The use of paint in nibs is discussed in a later chapter.

The most expensive papers are not always the best for calligraphy. Special practice pads, which have slope lines drawn, may be purchased. However, a guideline sheet, with the appropriate slope lines, may be ruled up and placed under bank typing paper, layout pad paper, good quality exercise book or file paper. Guidelines can then be easily seen.

For finished work, any paper that the nib will glide over freely may be used. It should not, however, be too highly glazed, or the nib will slip and be hard to control. Letter strokes must also remain crisp, and the ink must not spread between the fibres to give a hairy look. If the paper has a tendency for ink spread, spraying it with charcoal or pastel drawing fixative may help. Treatment with powdered gum sandarac is a useful alternative and is described for the treatment of vellum in a later chapter.

It is usually necessary for one to rest the writing hand on a piece of paper, a guard sheet, over the finished work. This stops grease and perspiration from one's fingers getting into the grain of the paper, and stopping the ink from penetrating properly.

There are many types of ink specially made for calligraphy, but these should be restricted to use on finished works. For practice, most people use an inexpensive washable fountain pen ink. Preferably this should be black as it shows errors more clearly. Only non-waterproof inks should be used as waterproof ones contain shellac, which dries in pens & clogs them with a type of varnish.

Each brand has its devotees, but the selection depends largely on the speed of one's writing and personal preference. Good brands include Higgins, Pelikan, Winsor and Newton, Calli, Osmiroid and Speedball. When experience has been gained stick ink, rubbed with a few drops of purified water on an ink slab to just the right consistency, should be freshly prepared for each piece of writing. However, the Chinese stick inks have such beautiful designs on them that it usually seems a shame to use them.

4· ·Foundational·Hand·

A roundhand calligraphic style has been chosen to start with, based on Edward Johnston's Foundational Hand, which he developed from his studies of 10th century Carolingian manuscripts, in particular the Ramsey Psalter. Apart from being attractive in its own right, competence in this script helps when other alphabets are approached. It can be easily modified into a Humanistic script and has flexibility for compression and being written at an angle. In this way, Johnston developed his Italic writing style.

1. Foundational Hand
2. Compressed Foundational Hand
3. Italic

In Foundational hands, verticals cut through both thinnest parts of o. In Italic the axis of an oval o is sloped. The downstrokes cut off both outer edges of o, and are less sloped, creating the characteristic 'branching arches'.

The ideal writing position is with the light coming from the left, with one's feet on the ground and back supported. Writing should always be done on a hard sloping surface (about 30 - 40 degrees is usually comfortable). If a board on a stand is not available, it can be rested on a heavy object, for example a brick wrapped in paper. Later it may be useful to make a stand at a fixed angle. One which overlaps the edge of the desk and has a rounded lower edge, helps to prevent the paper from being creased. A piece of card, taped to the bottom edge of the board so that it overhangs is an alternative.

Right-handed people should find that they write comfortably where, looking straight ahead of them, their eyes meet the board at right angles. To start with, the whole arm should preferably be used for drawing letters, or at least the whole hand, with minimal use of the fingers.

Left handed people often find that the most comfortable writing spot is to the left of their left shoulder. Their pen should then point to the left shoulder, and the writing paper may need to be angled.

When a comfortable position has been found, tape a small pad of newspaper about 10 cm (4 in) square and four sheets thick to the board. This will act as a slightly softer

area for writing and, by moving
the writing paper, and only writing

within this
square, it will
be easier to keep
the pen angle
constant, and vertical lines vertical.
In this alphabet, the thinnest lines
will always be at

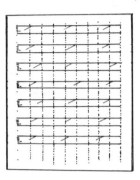

30 degrees to the horizontal
(PEN ANGLE), and the

PEN ANGLE
Thinnest line

thickest ones at right angles to the
thinnest ones. Thick and thin lines are produced by the
direction the pen moves in only, controlled not by pressure, by
twisting the pen or the wrist. Different scripts require a differ
ent pen angle, but the angle is kept constant in all movements in any one given style.

Rule guidelines 4½ nib widths apart, and mark 30 degree
lines in various places so that pen angle may be easily check-
ed as you go across and down the page, as shown in the diagram above. Feint vertical lines also help in keeping letter
strokes upright. These can be drawn on every sheet written
on, or a ruled sheet can be placed under the working sheet so
that they can be seen through it.

Adjust pen, writing position and paper until the pen
lines up with the 30 degree marks, and the following

patterns can be produced:-

Pull the pen down the paper, or slide it from side to side on thin strokes. NEVER PUSH THE PEN. Move the paper as the edge of your newspaper square is reached.

Using a compass, draw circles nearly to fill the the writing lines down the left side of the paper. When the letter O is drawn in the following way, it should fill the writing lines. One feature of this script is that each edge of the pen traces a circle but it is easiest, while learning, to concentrate on the centre of the nib following the circle.

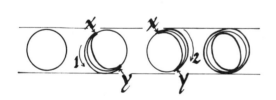

Start at (x), where the pen makes it's thinnest mark, move at even speed and stop at (y), where the thinnest mark is again made. Make a precise halt for half a second at the end of the stroke before taking the pen vertically from the paper. This will ensure a crisp finish to letters. Go back to (x) and draw the pen in the opposite direction for the other half of the letter. Having left (x), the centre of the nib should follow the circle until point (y) is reached, where again the whole nib should rest on the circle. The outside of the o will be slightly larger than a circle, and the inside shape slightly oval.

Practice many more o's round compass lines, then without. Always use top and bottom guide lines, however. Writing large helps you to minimise finger movement, and the widest pen you possess should be selected at the start, or even two pencils taped together.

For the heads of letters with ascenders – b, d, h, k and l, – a serif is required. Most calligraphers :-

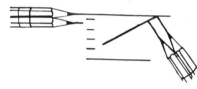

1. construct part of a small circle – about ¼

2. Remove the pen from the paper. From the starting point, slide the pen along a thin line for 2 nib widths, pause, then pull the pen vertically down for the rest of the stroke.

The tails of p's and q's may initially be left square ended (1). Later, additions may be made by pulling the last tiniest fraction of the stroke to the left by the smallest possible amount, then drawing

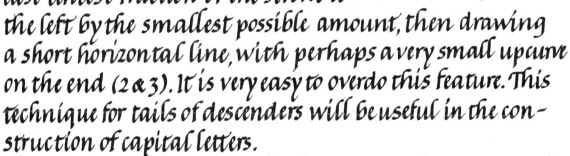

a short horizontal line, with perhaps a very small upcurve on the end (2 & 3). It is very easy to overdo this feature. This technique for tails of descenders will be useful in the construction of capital letters.

Apart from o there is another letter from which many other

letters of the alphabet are built. That is the letter i. It may start like the top of an ascender, or the circular portion used at the start may be made continuous with a vertical stroke. The curve at the bottom of the letter is part of a slightly smaller circle than an o. It starts curving at about the same level that an o has its thinnest point on the right-hand side. As soon as as the thinnest mark starts to be formed, stop, then remove the pen from the paper. The dot can be a small diamond or comma, though something in between is a personal favourite.

A knowledge of the construction of n also aids in the drawing of many other letters. The upper part of the left hand limb is the same as that of an i. At the bottom of the vertical, the curve of the serif stroke is reversed, with minimal thin line.

The curved top is part of an o, and starts changing thickness straight away, so there is no portion of thin line showing. The pen should be matched to cover the vertical, and then the curve drawn from there. The vertical on the right cuts the o through its thinnest part on the lower

34

right-hand side. The ending of the second is larger than that of the first limb, terminating like an i. As experience in writing is gained the size of these feet will be varied slightly. It is good to keep them all the same size when learning individual letters, but eventually placement of letters in words demands optically even spacing. When letters need to be close together the curve may be reduced:

ni no na

When letters need to be separated slightly, the curve can become larger to still give the appearance of joined letters, even though the letters are constructed singly.

The building of other letters is shown in the following diagrams. The order of strokes should be carefully followed. To help relate letters to the O shape, where appropriate, O's can be drawn on an underlay beneath the practice sheet. The aim should be to construct a row of five perfect examples of each letter.

flatten the top   tuck in   flattish top

equal areas

Steepen the pen angle
on the second stroke of v
& similar strokes of w.

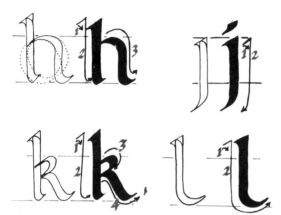

flattened
top

version·1

When writing words, the area between letters should look the same as the area within letters. This takes much practice. The space between words should be kept small, certainly no larger than a letter o.

fromotrain

rv   Sometimes letter shapes can be compressed to keep areas looking constant.

li loom

Parallel vertical strokes should always remain well spaced. When two curves come together they may nearly touch. The distance between a vertical and a curve will be between these two extremes. Many letters can be placed close enough for the finishing stroke of one letter to join the next.

When correctly shaped letters have been mastered with a wide nib, smaller writing can then be attempted – still 4½ nib widths high for minuscules. At first, writing lines should be kept just so far apart that p's on one line do not meet d's on the next line. One will soon start to formulate

ones own ideas on layout and design, but further help is
is provided in later chapters. Remember that the crispest
letter shapes are formed when, at the end of each stroke, the
pen pauses on the paper and then is removed vertically. Watching the size and shape of the counter, the white space inside
each letter, also helps in producing the best letter forms.

  A study of the proportions of carved Roman capitals
enables good pen made examples to be drawn.
There is a temptation to make capitals
too tall. 6~6½ nib widths is sufficient,
coming below the level of ascenders.

Th

A A A A B B B

B B C D D E

E F G H H I I

JJKLLL

The thin lines are drawn from the wet ink with the nib corner

MMNN

steepened pen angle

OPPQRRS

change angle

TTUVWW

WXXYYZ

This version has been written in the flavour of Johnston's original pattern

A wide curve to start serifs

Large blocks Prominent v's

Version·2

abcdefghi
jklmnopqr
stuvwxyz

The size and shape of the serifs is closer to the 10th century scripts in many cases.

ABCDEFG
HIJKLMNO

40

PQRSTUV
WXYZ

12345 *Note the alternate ups and downs* 6789

The original scripts from which Foundational Hand was developed were more complex in their construction. However, it is always useful to study original manuscripts in museum or library collections (or very good photographs of them) and analyse them. The size of writing, ascenders and descenders in nib widths; the pen angle most used, and any variations; and the shape of basic letters (e.g. letter o and how this relates to other letters), are characteristics which should be noted. One should also note what order of strokes was used; the shape of serifs; the slope of letters or parts of letters; spacing between words and lines and the proportions of the margins around the page and the script. One should also look at features of letters and try to decide if they were produced painstakingly, or if they indicate the manuscript was written at speed. The size of the original, and the type of pen and materials used should also be established. Such an analysis helps train us to be aware of these important characteristics, as we learn any script that we choose to copy, or that we design ourselves.

In many manuscripts studied, not all letters of the modern alphabet were in use and others may not have been required for the given text. The Ramsey Psalter in the British Museum on which Johnston based his Foundational Hand has a manuscript number – Harley 2904. The size of letters is about 5 mm (3/16 in). The illustration is an attempt to analyse the script and design 'missing letters. with the same flavour. It is possible to see that Johnston retained the strong arch shapes and modified the a and g, for example, to try to make them stronger for larger writing heights

One feature of this manuscript is the the apparent joy of the scribe in its execution, which comes through in the fluidity of the writing. This cannot be learnt, but develops as letter shapes become second nature until there is little doubt that, when written, they will have all the desired characteristics.

Foundational Hand, like the original, may be written only 4 pen widths high, giving the text a heavier feel.

· ſ·ONE two ·ſ one two·

b dm̃: ꝑequando rap

non ſit

h

m

i

Harley

f. 2904

z s k

d l l i

the original
height of
letters ·5mm

w v

l i

30°

arguam te & fta

contra faciem t

Blessed are the

From Christ's sermon on the mount

poor in spirit

Versal capitals, painted or in gold, may also be used effectively ❦ ❦ ❦

Many of the humanistic manuscripts were in this size of script

The Humanistic scripts developed in Italy in the 15th and 16th centuries resulted from the study of the the earlier Caroline Minuscules. Many were written only 2½ - 3mm (¹⁄₁₆ - ⅛ in.) high. & the shapes of many serifs and stroke finishes were produced by twisting the quill and probably pressure changes too. The letter shapes provided the inspiration for the Roman type face. A similar appearance to this script may be created by adding square feet to Foundational, and the serifs at the heads of letters may be squared a little too. Pen-made or pencil drawn and brush painted versions of Roman capitals are most appropriate with Humanistic Roman styles, though narrow not too exaggerated versals can be used.

abcdefghijklmn
opqrstuvwxyyz

ABCDEFGHIJK
LMNOPQRSTU
Modern VWXYZ Alphabet

PERFECTLY·DRAWN

PEN MADE LETTERS, WELL SPACED
were used for headings. The capitals drawn in the text were tiny,
like the minuscules, for the most part. At the beginning of a new
section of text, capitals were just over twice the size of the minuscules
and more shaping of the serif completed with the corner of the
nib. Versal letters, with slight exaggeration of proportions, were used
too.

A B C D E F G
H I J K L M N
O P Q R S T
U V W X Y Z

The alphabet drawn above is based on the letter forms found in 15th century Humanistic manuscripts. Each letter is built according to the principles shown below. Pen angles are often changed between and during strokes, and wet ink at the termination of strokes is pulled by the corner of the nib to construct or fill in the serifs.

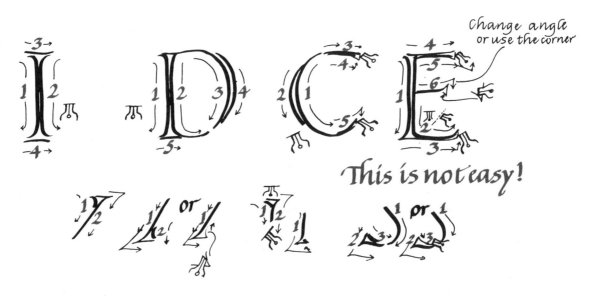

This is not easy!

Similar methods may be used to produce pen made versions of the Roman capital letters described in Chapter 2. This is useful because it is often easiest to lay gesso, or raising preparation, with a pen prior to attaching gold.

compression of Foundational Hand gives an impression of solidity

Compression of Foundational Hand gives a heavy effect. The principles of construction remain the same, but the arch radius to letter height ratio is altered.

The transition from the Carolingian style to the Gothic form of writing followed from compression of the Caroline minuscules, with heavier serifs on the heads and feet. The final Gothic script increased the angularity of the letter shapes and reduced the serifs to blocks.

Caroline

transition

Gothic

5. Setting·Out·a·Page

THE FIRST STEPS IN LAYOUT AND DESIGN

Once a first letter style has been well practised, there will be a desire to write out a chosen text. There are no hard and fast rules in layout and design. Ultimately, individuality will arise from one's own taste and judgement, but it is useful to experience, by observation and experimentation a variety of ideas and techniques. This chapter provides some simple ideas. It is best not to attempt to use the most demanding equipment or the more complex designs, until confidence in basic skills is attained. The simplest designs are often the most stunning anyway.

Experiments and rough copies are necessary. One aim of rough copies is to determine how long a particular line of writing will be. Therefore they must be written with care. Letter collisions between one line and the next can also be avoided, often by making ascenders & descenders shorter than usual at these places.

STAGE 1   1. To begin with, choose a short
    SUGGESTIONS   piece of work to write out – for exam-

ple, a two or three line saying – then progress to longer texts

2. When a rough copy has been written, cut it into separate lines of writing, and, if necessary, cut these up again so that they can be juggled on the table until a pleasing design is found. Then tape or stick them to a piece of paper in this layout. The title is usually added last.

A friend is
someone who knows
all about you ...
but likes you anyway

A friend is someone
who knows all about you ...
but likes you anyway

A friend is someone
who knows all about you ...
but likes you anyway.

3· When writing in any script initially keep flourishes above the top line, below the bottom line, and at the ends of lines only.

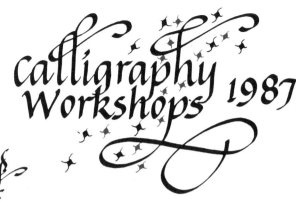

Paper and text areas are the same

4· Choose a piece of paper that the completed work will fit on easily with a large amount of space left all around for margins. The more space that is left around each edge of a text, the more important that text will look.

a word ⌐x height 5· Mark the position of the first line with a pencil, as two dots for the 'x' height of minuscules.

6· Whatever this height is, multiply it by 1½. This will be the distance from the bottom of the top line of writing to the top of

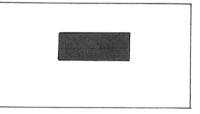

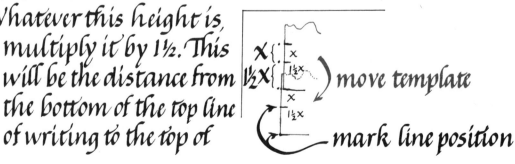

) move template

mark line position

the second line. This position is marked.

7. Mark all three positions on a piece of scrap paper, and use this as a template to mark the line heights and spaces between lines for the rest of the text.

8. Use a drawing board or square, if available, to rule the lines. However, the lines of commercially ruled paper placed underneath may provide a guide, or a piece of paper with a square corner, placed on top, can also enable ruling to be easily accomplished.

9. If the paper to be written on is thin, commercially ruled file paper can be used as a visible underlay to show vertical guide lines, or these may be drawn over the top to keep writing at the desired angle.

Don't Forget to use a guard sheet under your hand, to help prevent grease and perspiration affecting the paper.

When you have dipped a pen into ink, wipe it, then test it on a scrap sheet to see if it contains the right amount of ink. Thin lines should be fine, and thick strokes should have crisp square ends.

STAGE 2
SUGGESTIONS

10. Study the proportion of border to text on originals or photographs of work that you admire done by other people. Some traditional proportions are as follows

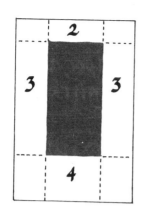

A single
sheet

An open
book

For pages in the ratio
3:4 (short side : long)
try these, then
change the

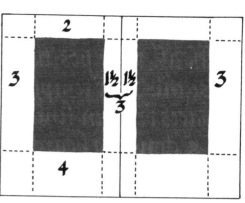

proportions a little, if desired, to suit your
own taste.

The margin
widths are
in 1/16ths of
the longest
side of a
page.

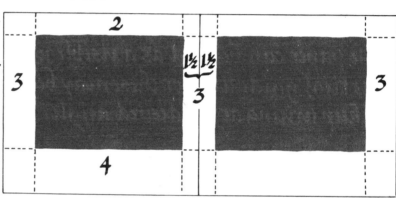

11· When writing prose, try to make lines of writing more
than five words long, preferably between seven and
fourteen on average.

12· Study the effect when spacing between lines is increased and decreased. A slightly wider spacing of lines is
usually more pleasing for poems than for prose.

13· Experiment with adding colour. One of the earliest,
and still most impressive combination, is black and.
A calligraphic felt pen, or coloured ink is a convenient way of seeing what the completed work may

look like. However, for the finished copy, red gouache paint is preferred, because it is denser and more fade resistant. The paint is mixed with water until, when the mixing dish is tilted, it will just trickle freely down the side. It must be thin enough to leave the nib, like ink, but not contain so much water that the colour of the paper shows through.

Trial and error experimentation is necessary. Winsor and Newton's Scarlet Lake or Flame Red are the ones that I use most. Traditionally a rubricator would add the red letters to a manuscript in Vermillion. This colour is very expensive. In Chapter 12 the use of color is further described.

LOVE·ME
MOST
WHEN·I
DESERVE
IT·LEAST·
THAT'S·WHEN
I·NEED
IT·MOST·

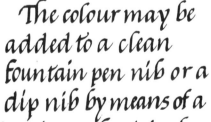

The colour may be added to a clean fountain pen nib or a dip nib by means of a brush, scraping it on the side of the nib from the underside towards the front.

Each time a pen is loaded, it should be tested to make sure that the letters drawn will be crisp.

Some ways that red can be used include ~

 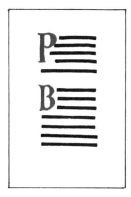 

a· The title

b·The first letter (often two or more lines high, & drawn as a versal letter). See Chapter 10.

c· The first word or few words, may be in capitals

d· For a large work, the first paragraph may be in red (or the last one)

e· All capitals throughout the work could be rubricated, or all capitals starting the separate verses of a poem.

f· Stave lines in music

g· Decorative line endings and fill-in devices

Another good colour that may be used is blue. A mixture to start with is Ultramarine with a touch of Permanent White. Alternating red and blue capitals to start the verses of poems can be useful, or a blue capital at the start of a text, followed by smaller red capitals then black writing.

14· Try a 'scroll pen' or shadow nib to produce hollow letters, may be for a title or initial capital.

STAGE 3
SUGGESTIONS

15· Try writing with different sized nibs. Use them to create different heights of writing. With some poems, for example, one verse, or a chorus, can be placed between the lines of a different verse. This is useful where ideas are separate, and can be done in small writing possibly in a different colour. Another use is for different emphases, for example, a poet's name is usually written smaller than the verses, and a firm's name is written larger than their address on their letterhead.

Verse one · verse one ·
Verse two · verse two

Verse one · verse one ·
Verse two · verse two

Verse one · verse one ·
Verse two · verse two

16. Study how to add gold to a manuscript, and choose decorations and a decorative capital that blends with the writing style. These topics are fully dealt with in later chapters.

**Many strokes
though with a little axe
Hew down & fell
the**

the hardest timbered oak

17. Try to produce some writing which is perfectly balanced at each side of a centre line.

a. Write a good rough copy in the same sized writ-ing as the finished copy.

b. Measure the length of each line and mark its centre point.

c. Rule up the finished sheet and mark a centre line.

d. Fold the rough copy between each line of writing.

e. Each line of writing on the rough copy is laid, in turn, under the appropriate pair of guidelines, with with its centre spot on the centre line.

f. The rough is used as a guard sheet under the hand as the text is copied above it to fit in the same space.

There are problems that have to be faced when

writing invitations to be folded. These are dealt with in Chapter 12.

18. Write and bind a small single section book — maybe one or two verses of a poem on each page, or a fable, or a short piece of prose, up to about six page sides. The binding method is described below.

a. Write a good rough copy of the text to determine how much space will be needed.

b. Fold some scrap paper and write on each page what will be contained in the finished book.

c. Choose a suitable paper and fold it in the direction of the grain for easy opening & flatness. The paper is chosen to open flat under its own weight after having been creased.

cover
endpapers
verses 4 & 5
verses 2 & 3
verse 1
title
endpapers
cover of manilla card or similar

sheet buckles when your fingernails are drawn across the grain at right angles to it.

Sheet remains smooth when your fingernails are drawn along the grain.

d. Mark out writing lines and margin widths to try to establish a pleasing visual appearance.

Some margin proportions have already been suggested for books where the sides are in the ratio of 3:4. If the page dimensions are closer to 2:3, the margins may look better with proportions around 1/16 th of the longest side for each inner margin, 2/16ths for the fore-edge,1½/16ths on the top, and 3/16 ths on the bottom, though ultimately this will change in relation to personal taste. Many people decrease the size of the inner margins in particular. Remember that, when sewn together, the edges will receive a slight trim, and allow for this.

e. Write the pages before sewing the book.

f. If considering using gold, beware that in humid climates gum ammoniac gilding may become sticky and glue pages together, particularly if it is raised. Gilded areas should not meet on opposite pages when the book is closed.

g. The pages and cover are pierced, as shown, prior to sewing with linen thread. The diagram below shows the path of the thread. It must be tightened, however, by pulling only in the direction that the thread has just come from, then tied with the long piece between the two ends. The thread when cut, may be frayed and pressed, with the knot, into a butterfly shape.

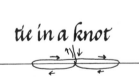

tie in a knot

knot

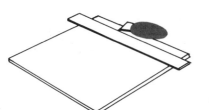

h. The pages and cover are trimmed together.

The following method describes how to add a paper cover that will not slip off, even though it may not be permanently attached. One beauty of such covers is the great variety of means that can be used to add a title and decoration. Apart from calligraphy with a pen, embossing, intaglio and other methods of printing can be used, along with most artistic media.

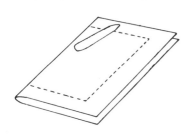

i. Cut your cover paper so that, when folded, it will extend about 2-3 cm (1–1¼ in) above and below the book block, and about one third the width of the book beyond the fore-edge. The cover may be left loose, or it may be attached with a 5 mm (¼ in) strip of glue on the back cover next to the spine. Lay the book spine in the crease of the cover paper. Run a folder around all book edges to mark the cover paper at the extremities of the book block.

j. Fold the paper cover along the marks defining the fore-edge, and crease well with a folder. It is best to lay one or two sheets of clean paper over the work to be rubbed with the folder, to prevent the appearance of shiny marks. Cut the top and bottom edges of the cover paper flush with the book block and covers. MOST IMPORTANT OF ALL, leave a quarter of a circle at the corners. I usually draw around a twenty-cent coin for this.

k. The book is then opened up. Each projecting corner semicircle can be folded under the raised cover flap, and over the outer end paper. The large flap can be cut decoratively if desired.

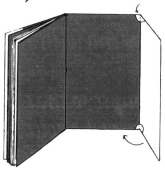

6. ·Gothic·

The compression and angularity of Gothic writing gives the text a 'heavy' look, and with close lines of writing the page develops an impression of black stripes making up a solid whole. The spontaneity of the early forms in 12th and 13th centuries, with somewhat complex structure, turned to more mechanical letter forms in the Textura versions of the 15th century. This style of writing has lost favour as we have become used to reading more rounded scripts, and now find it hard to interpret. However, the possibilities for creating texture and interesting designs on the page using Gothic are considerable, & it can be used in small measure with other styles.

hijkl
mnop
qrstuv
wx
yz

62

A simple version of Textura Gothic is described initially to enable the rhythms present in all Gothic styles to be developed, and as a foundation for the more complex variations. A very large book could be devoted to such ancient and modern varieties, but some historic examples have been selected and a modernised version described in detail.

The height of letters as measured by nib widths is probably more flexible in Gothic styles than in any other script. A good height for the 'x' height of letters is 5 nib widths to start with.

Ascenders and descenders extend about 2½ nib widths either side, and capitals total about 6½ nib widths.

The pen angle is maintained at about 40 degrees at all times, and all strokes are produced by pulling the pen or sliding sideways to make the thinnest marks.

To check the pen angle, a vertical cross may be drawn. The horizontal will only be a tiny fraction thinner than the upright.

0 **0,0,0,0**
1 2 3 4 5 6

The aim is to make the space inside each letter, the counter, look the same. If this does not happen it will be necessary to adjust the block size or block angle.

1. Standard width of letter.
2. Blocks too small.
3. Blocks too large and not parallel.
4. Blocks of different sizes.
5. Blocks too large and rather flat.
6. Blocks too steep.

Letters are constructed by the following methods:—

1. A small starting movement to get ink along the edge of the nib.

40°   40°

2. Construct the block — about 1⅓ times longer than the width of the pen nib. Pause and remove the nib vertically for a crisp ending.

3. Replace the nib precisely back on the block so that, when it is drawn downwards the centre of the nib passes through the lower corner of the block.

4. The lower block is parallel to the top one. The nib is repositioned with its centre on the left hand edge of the vertical, and the same size of block created.

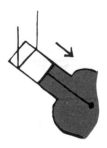

An 'i' shape is thus produced. Elements of this, or of 'o', are used to build most other letters.

The 'o' starts with two nib widths of thin line, then moves into the bottom half of 'i'. The pen is rematched on to the one nib-width of thin line left at the top, & top half of 'i' constructed. The lower corners should meet perfectly. A thin diagonal line can be used to close any gaps.

abcdefghij

no 'tick' stroke

Note that all verticals are truly vertical. The tops of a, c, g, and q are flattened. The top of 'e' is sloped downwards more than the blocks of other letters. The top of 'd' crosses below the guideline

ALTERNATIVE 'a'
use the nib corner

65

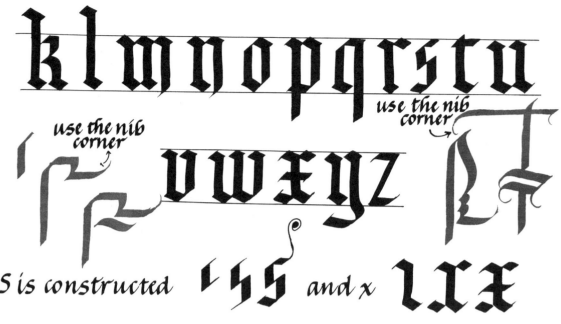

k l m n o p q r s t u

use the nib corner

use the nib corner

v w x y z

S is constructed ʿ ȿȿ and x ʟɪx

A 14th century manuscript fragment shows an alternative x which may be simp-lified to —

Actual Size 23mm (15/16 in)

iu replebuntur mguestent speao et exultatione co entur.

Capitals present many problems. Originally most capitals were drawn as versals in paint, or gilded. Detailed constructions are given in Chapter 10. This is a good method to maintain throughout, with fine decoration, if desired.

Dominus uobiscum. et ru duo Requetna sancti lu secundum lucam. Glo

28mm (1⅛ in)

unt. Mare co o plantus et rebunt. Terra ia co mouen t. Sol cogno

22mm (⅞ in)

Many of the pen-made capitals in the 13th and 14th centuries were very small to match the writing size used, and one cannot presume

66

that they will look as effective when enlarged. Most of
the complex Old English letters used by printers cannot
be written adequately with a pen, as they were designed by engravers, or cut as woodblocks.

Designing capitals to match Gothic
styles can give rise to much ornamentat-
ion and variation. Hairlines and diamo-
nds may be added in red, too, for example.
However, the most important feature
must be readability. The selection
provided is a starting point. Each calligraphy book
will give a different version, but ultimately you will
design your own.

Turn the pen for (or use the corner)
thin lines

A B C D E F G

h I J K L M N O P Q

R S T U V W X Y Z

A B C D E F G
H I J K L M N O
P Q R S T U V
V W W F X Y Z

←Start alternatives

For titles, or at other times when a whole word needs
to be in capitals, the use of versals is recommended.
The numerals present problems too. Roman

1 2 3 4 5 6 7 8 9 0

numerals probably match the letter shapes best, but are not always a viable proposition. Those drawn may act as a starting point for experimentation.

When writing words, the space between letters should be the same as the space inside letters, so that after a letter r, c, e, t or x, the top **minimum** **rig** block of the next letter may need to be reduced in size. The space between words need only be a fraction wider than the space between letters.

Neer linger, Neer o'er hasty be, for time moves on with measured foot.

~ Goethe ~

Because a dense appearance is generated in this style, it is also usual to make the space between lines close. This can be reduced to less than the x height of letters, to produce a unity in the finished piece. Much of the beauty of the early manuscripts is a result of consistency, , but also due to fluency and the speed at which they were written. Letter shapes were often a mixture of curves and angular blocks. However, these were used in a highly controlled fashion, e.g. on the last stroke of an m or n, but not on the earlier strokes.

The curved hair lines suggest a rapid flicking of the quill and may have been done with the corner. The corner was certainly used to extend hairlines from top of ascenders.

6 cm
(2 5/16 in) 14th century

Though the corners of blocks extend in n, m, & u, they show much less on o and e, for example.

It may be noted that some letters share limbs. This practice is particularly useful when line lengths have to remain constant.

A hair separates the elements of many letters, but the top of e, and bottom of p, overlap the earlier strokes to make thickened corners.

The bottom of o, b and d tend to be drawn at a flatter angle than the lower blocks of other letters.

These subtleties give this manuscript its character; however, one must be aware that changes of letter size may well require different techniques.

Textura and other highly angular Gothic styles were

largely limited to Northern Europe. In Spain & Italy, Rotunda maintained much of the strong rhythm of other Gothic forms, but with many rounded shapes.

compression of letters also features in this alphabet, though capitals were often wide. Although Rotunda was used in very small books, the original 17th century leaves that these notes were made from are large — one measures 82 cm x 57 cm (32 x 22½ in).

Philiberti ab
extv
puenisti. Alia.
ccv
cõsfidelis ser,
offin. Salus

|← 8 cm →|
(3¼ in)

The alphabet construction is more complex than it would first appear. Though different scribes have always developed their own techniques, the following appear to have been used by medieval professionals. It will be left to the reader to develop his or her own dexterity, to produce a 20th century version with a similar flavour. It has to be considered, however, that

it was the niceties of pen angle changes and pen manipulations used, that gave the original an important part of it's true character.

14·5cm
(5¾in)

Note the horizontal pen angle for the start of vertical strokes. The angle is changed for the downstroke, with a protruding corner at the top. However, whilst the pen is in motion it is twisted at the last fraction of the stroke to form a flat end and a small triangular mark on the bottom right-hand corner. Note also the overlap on the top of e.

Darker lines in the fading ink show that the pen was removed after the angular stroke at the top of m,

and the angle changed, then the downstroke drawn.

72

ox sancti

VERSION·2

This manuscript leaf is in two parts. This very formal script between stave lines has a very gradual pen angle change from top to bottom of vertical strokes, producing a tapered look. These are completed by a movement of the pen to the right. O and e do not over-lap at the corners. Many curves, like c, change to a more shallow pen angle during the down stroke to form a fine, low, exit. The tops of many vertical strokes start

bartholo

with a horizontal pen angle. Apparently the right hand corner stayed in its starting position until a twist had brought the nib to its normal writing angle, and a small triangular extension had been created on the top left hand corner.

Joy and speed in writing is suggested by the sweeping curved strokes on x and s, and the hairline on top of i.

75

In another section of the page, in a block of massed writing, the serif shapes are more angular extensions of the limbs of the letters. The original minuscules & capitals are printed in black. Where these original forms appear weak or not easily readable a suggestion for a modernised form has been added. Similarly, where particular letters are not present on the original manuscript, a design with the same flavour is offered. Versal capitals were also used, as were those of a heavy woven design.

r a b c d e f g h i

j k l m n o p q r

s t u v w x y z

A B B C D E

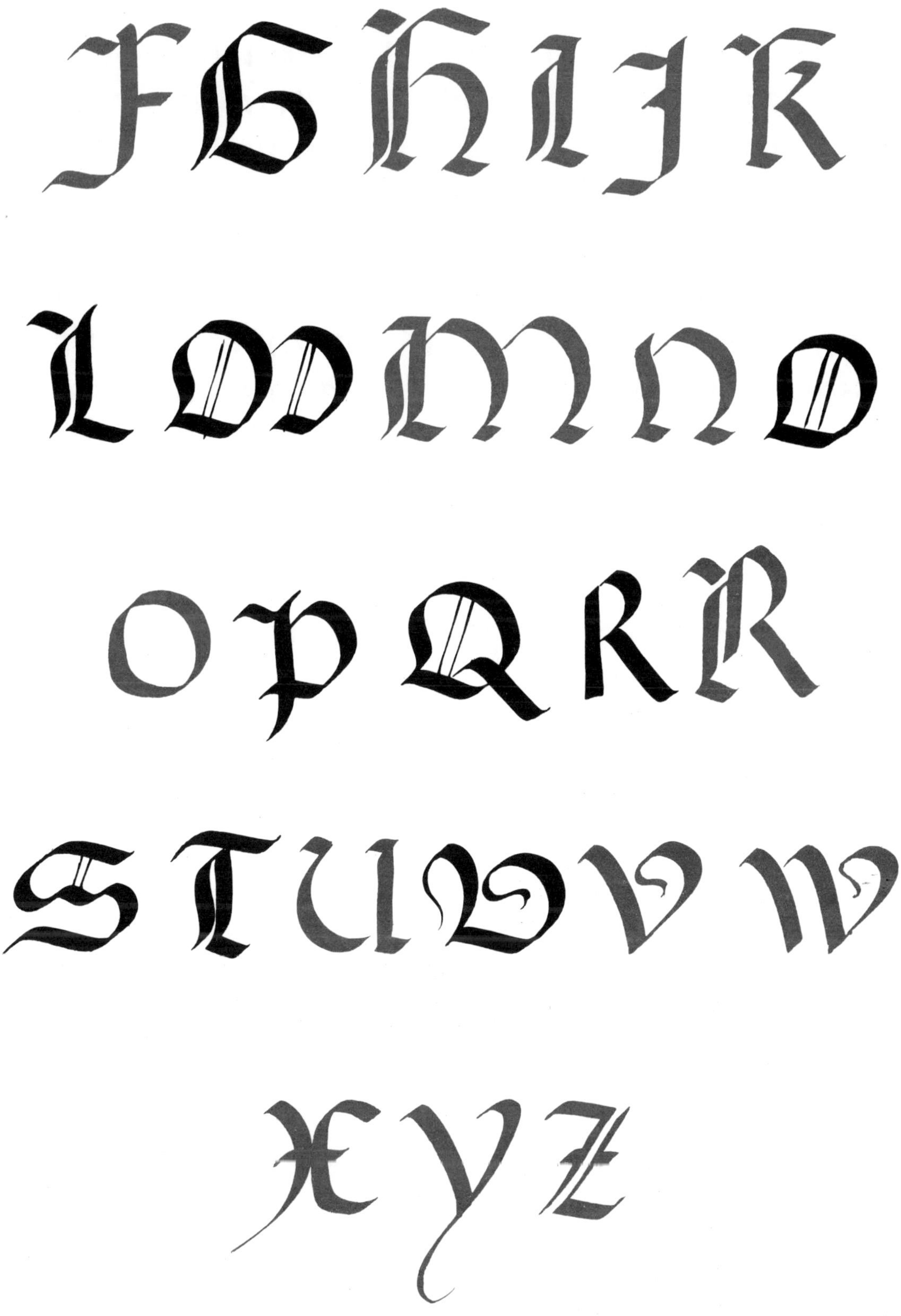

FGHIJK

LMMNO

OPQRR

STUVVVW

XYZ

75

A detailed study of a piece of ancient writing helps in the copying of exemplars and styles of modern scribes whose work may be shown in books. It may also help in designing alphabets or modifying to one's own taste.

The Rounded Gothic style in detail in the rest of this chapter is an attempt to create an alphabet with compressed letters, which are easily readable, and built on family resemblances. It can be used successfully for very formal writing but has a form that allows its use in poems and prose.

As in other alphabets, the shape of the o determines the structure of other letters in the style.

The 'x' height of letters is 4½–5 times the width of the nib used, and the pen angle is about 65 degrees.

Imagine each half of o to be part of a larger smooth circle. Stop crisply on the line, pause, and remove the pen vertically. The top and bottom apices should be in a vertical line.

Match the pen up again at the top, and add the right hand half to join precisely at the bottom of the first stroke – wait for a second – remove the pen.

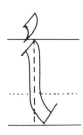

Letter i starts with the pen sliding upwards 1½ nib-widths to the top line. Halt. Start the right hand side of an o, but as soon as the left hand side of the nib reaches the starting level, draw the pen vertically. The bottom curve is also part of o, and starts ⅓rd of the letter height from the bottom line. A vertical line from the top apex bisects the vertical part of the letter.

For letter n, the vertical stroke starts as for an i. However, its lower extremity is the reverse of the top, only without the thin. Although it is still the bottom fraction of an o, the right-hand side of the nib should start moving from the vertical no more than ¼ of the letter height from the base line. The thin line to start the right-hand side of the letter joins the vertical ¼ of the letter height from the upper guide line. If the thin is longer than 1½ nib widths when it reaches the guide line, check the pen angle, or start it higher. Make a halt at the top line before adding the right half of an o. Do not extend it more than ½ a nib width below the guide line at this stage.

Most letters of the alphabet contain part of an o, i

or n.

Tops
of b,d,h,k,l :

1. As the top of i.

OR

2. Start with a curve. Add a short thin, then a downstroke.

Tails
of p and q

1. Start with the tiniest movement left, then pull the pen horizontally with a minute upturned tip. Magnified:

For g, pay.

OR

3. Start with a small curve.
   Add a top curving downwards, the width of the letter.
   — Use the nib corner.

These flourishes are for 'special occasions'.

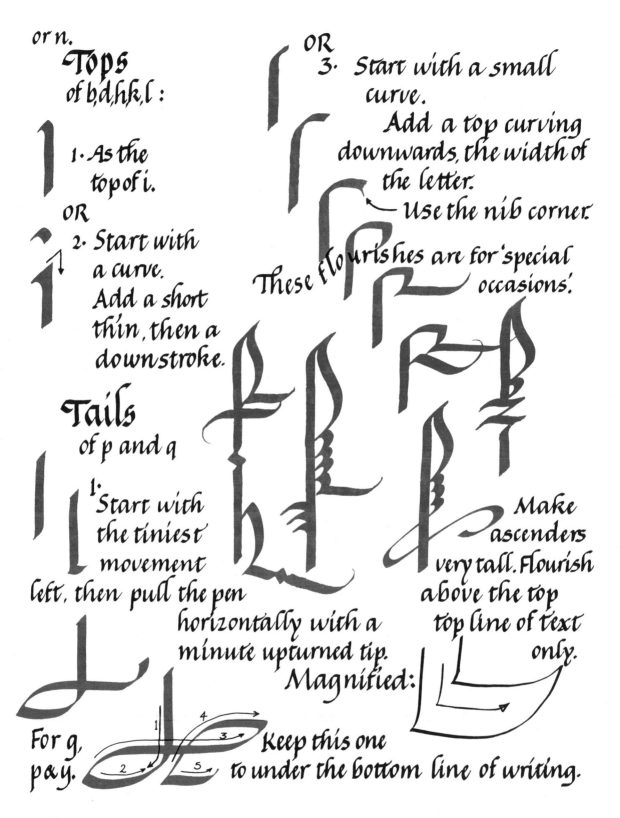

Make ascenders very tall. Flourish above the top top line of text only.

Keep this one to under the bottom line of writing.

78

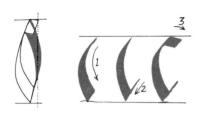

The relationship between
c, e, and o is obvious. The thin
on the bottom should be no
longer than 1 nib width.

The top of c can be straight, but inclining
slightly downwards from the horizontal.
It is not part of the o. The top of e tucks
inwards. In both c and e, you should be able to draw a
vertical line from top to bottom extremities on the right.

l is a tall letter i without the dot.
The height of this and h and k is 1½
writing lines. b and d are
fractionally shorter.

d is started
with half an o
The thin added can be
longer than for c or e, because
the l added can cut some off ~ ½-1 nib width should
remain ~ not more. The bottom curve added to the
vertical starts its o shaped curve immediately the
thin is reached and should be identical with the lower
left side. Line 5 is straight and horizontal,
or sloping downhill a tiny fraction.

An alternative d is an o with a longer second
stroke. This is straight until the start of the o is
reached. The cross over point is below the top line.

79

 As with d, the a starts with half an o, and an added thin to the bottom. The straight top may then be drawn, a little more downhill than on d if desired. The right-hand i shape starts on the top line by sliding the pen down and left to make a minute curve to join with the top bar. As soon as the left-hand edge of the nib reaches the underside of the bar, the vertical is started. On reaching the thin, the o curve finishes the letter — again being identical to the lower 1/3 rd of the left-hand o stroke.

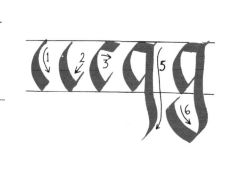 g is, perhaps, the most difficult letter. Strokes 1-3 are as for an a. Stroke 4 curves in a little, out a little, and in again. A confident smooth pen action is needed. Both halves of the bottom part are symmetrically wider than the top. The bottom area enclosed is greater than the top. A vertical line bisecting the bottom area should also bisect the top one.

  The left stroke of b is a slightly shortened l. When the thin is added under the top guide line, it should be 1½ nib widths long. When the

right-hand o shape completes the letter, ½ a nib width of thin line will then remain.

The structure of p is similar to b. It is usually best to complete the letter with a horizontal stroke. The tail length here is about ⅔rds of the top part.

q is simply a lengthened letter a.

h is a tall letter n. Don't forget, only a small curve at the bottom of the

vertical, with no tick stroke. The vertical of the k is as on the h — if anything, with an even smaller curve at the bottom. Stroke 2, the thin, is 2 nib widths long. The thin at the end of comma shaped stroke 3 must be parallel to the first thin. It need not join the vertical. The sloping stroke only curves as it touches the line, & ends outside the line of the curved top.

j starts like an i. The lower termination ends without any length of thin line showing.

The vertical of r is that of an n. The bar is angular & small.

81

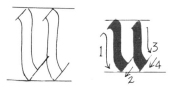

Letter u is two letter i's joining each other. The left-hand thin should be about 1/2 - 1 nib width long.

Start t 1 nib width below the writing line. Slide it 1 nib width above the line, then down vertically to complete the bottom of the i shape. The bar is short, and its top touches the writing line.

The height of f above the top line should be the same as that below the base line. Keep the top almost horizontal. The bottom curve will relate to the shape drawn for g. The middle bar is short, and lies with the top guideline resting on it. The left hand part is smaller than the part to the right of the vertical. Keep the bottom join angular. The top join can be a smooth curve.

m starts with the first stroke of an n. The second stroke starts like the second stroke of n; the vertical section starts when the left hand side of the nib reaches the level where the thin started. The third stroke is a repeat again, but the lower termination is the bottom shape of i.

82

To fit in with the rest of the script s must be narrow. Whilst drawing the letter, concentrate on the shape of the white space you are creating inside the letter. In both versions, the top is more horizontal than the lower limb, which starts outside the left edge.

The upper limb does not extend as far as the right-hand edge. The area enclosed by the top is a little smaller than at the bottom.

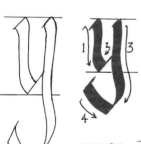

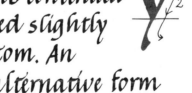

In v, line 1 does not quite touch the bottom line.

The pen angle is steepened for the thin diagonal to the line, and the little white gap touched in if necessary. W is two v's together. If the second stroke of the first v is not too curly at the top, the second v starts by overlapping this part.

y is a letter v with the second limb continued and curved slightly at the bottom. An alternative form is a u with a g-shaped tail, with a similar v and w.

It is difficult to make x narrow enough to match other letters. The base should be slightly wider than the top.

Make the base of z wider than the top. In this style, z must be kept narrow.

Another variation for the tails of g and y is to make them short and nearly horizontal. This is useful when writing lines are very close.

Other versions of capitals may be devised. They should relate to the minuscules, and a pointed nature is therefore needed. Versals can also be used, and when a word needs to be all in capitals, versals generally look better for this purpose.

Flourishes, too, reflect the angular nature of the script, and some examples have been provided. It will be found easier to construct them if ascenders are much longer than normal – up to 5 times the x height – and plenty of room is given to those on descenders. Where lines cross, try to do so boldly with no very small areas of white space formed, and only two lines crossing at any one point. Flourishes may also be added over capitals or other

white spaces too small

too many lines meeting, to give thick black areas

letters without ascenders, or under those without descenders, to balance a line of writing. However, it is important that an a is not made to look like a d or g, for example. A white gap is left between the flourish and the letter without an ascender or descender.

1 2 3 4 5 6 7 8 9 0 These are some ideas for numerals. Experiment!

As with all scripts, an even spacing of letters is aimed for, with the space between letters looking the same as the space inside letters. The thin exit strokes from letters can be used to join one letter to another.

shrill on those lofty
sloping leas
the wind bells sounded
in the breeze

When space available is a problem, the curved parts of adjoining letters may overlap. once

Transitional-
heavy serifs and
compressed

Quadrata-
square

Prescissus-
with square
ends

Gothic variations

Textura-
uniform
and block
serifs

Rotunda-
rounded

Rounded gothic-
a 20th century
alphabet

87

7 · · Italic ·

The styles that we recognise today as of an Italic nature derive much of their structure from the versions used in Italy in the 15th and 16th centuries. Many early manuscripts had few joins between letters, and formal Italic retains this characteristic of letters produced separately, though they may be closely written, and touch each other, to resemble a cursive or running script.

The development of Italic handwriting took place using the formal styles as a basis for letter shapes, but adding joins as a result of more rapid pen movements. Pope Eugenius IV apparently recognised the beauty in this script as used by Vatican scribes, and decreed that Papal Briefs should be written in this way. It became known as chancery cursive and was also adopted by educated laity, being widely used throughout Italy, Spain and beyond.

formal Italic   Italic handwriting

Writing masters, such as Arrighi, produced instruction manuals which were engraved and printed. Arrighi's 'Operina', printed in 1522, was cut in woodblocks. Unfortunately, it is not possible to engrave letters with the sharp but rounded turns that are produced by the pen, especially at the bottoms of letters like i. However, such manuals have provided much of the basis for the development of the alphabets of modern Italic writing masters. Calligraphers such as Alfred Fairbank, Irene Wellington, Tom Gourdie and Barbara Nichol, in particular, have done much work in the restyling of school scripts.

Many books have been written on the subject of Italic handwriting. Here an outline of letter shapes in a basic alphabet is provided, along with the principles upon which they are designed. They can be used formally, without running joins, but handwriting can be developed from them. A selection of flourishes and variations for experimentation are also given.

The characteristics of Italic writing which are important to achieve are compression of letters, branching arches, diagonal joins, and a strong 'bouncy' rhythm.

branching arch
diagonal
join exit
stroke
45°
Pen angle

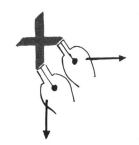

The pen angle is maintained at 45 degrees. Initially frequent checks should be made - perhaps by writing a vertical cross between letters. Both limbs of the cross should be the same width, with 45 degree ends. It may be easier to turn the paper to obtain this angle between nib edge and writing line, rather than change the way the pen is normally held.

The script has a slight forward lean - about 5 degrees - but this will not have to be thought about when a rhythm has become second nature. The 'x' height for most minuscules is 5 nib widths. Practice pads are available and are useful, as they have boxes drawn into which the letters fit.

The alphabet can be considered in families. The first family is related to a rhythm of anticlockwise pen movements, bouncing off the bottom line, with small tight curves and 45 degree exit strokes.

For the letter i, start with a tick stroke, make a sharp but curved turn at the bottom, and exit at 45 degrees. A small comma can be used for the dot.

The letter t has no starting stroke and is only about one nib width higher than i. The top writing line sits on the bar. Most of the bar is on the right, with only a corner

90

on the left.

The letter l is a tall i shape, 8 nib widths high.

For the letter v, make an i shape, but push the exit stroke uphill as it approaches the top line.

The letter w consists of two v's drawn all in one pen movement.

The letter u consists of a letter v with an i shaped second half. If properly formed it will be possible to write a capital A against the second vertical. Both lower apices will look the same.

To construct the letter a, it may be useful to imagine a clock face in a parallelogram. a is formed as a letter u with a top. The letter is started at 1, pushed very slightly uphill to 12, rounded gently to 9, then the rest of the u is completed. For d, the bowl is constructed first, then with a precise aim to cut through the corner, an l is added.

This construction may be easier with dip nibs and quills.

g is an a with a pointed tail. The tail of g is flattened at the base, and extends the width of the

PUSH
OR PULL

letter. If the paper is turned upside down it should be possible to match another g in the tail and top.

The letter y is a u with a g shaped tail. j is of similar shape, with a tick entry.

The top of f has the same shape as the top of a, and a tail to match g. The bar extends further to the right, and has the writing line on top of it. The extensions above and below the lines must look balanced, but don't make the letter too tall.

PUSH   OR PULL

The next series of letters are based on a clockwise rhythm. The nib leaves the bottom line, tracing a very short distance up the vertical, then branching at about 45 degrees until a tight turn is made at the top.

narrower wedge

In n, m and r, the starting stroke is curved, & parallel to the thin strokes of the arches.

These are the only three letters that start in this way. n a m terminate like an i.

The letter h has the same construction as n with a tall ascender.

b h b b

The letter b has the same branching structure and may be considered a q in reverse. The base has the tiniest of curves, as it is pushed into the vertical to complete it. Many find it easier to pull this stroke.

p

In making the letter p, the nib is removed at the end of the vertical and replaced on the lower guide line before constructing the bowl.

k k

The letter k requires a vertical stroke. Then, at the bottom of the vertical, branching like an n is needed, but making a tight turn at the top. It does not have to rejoin the vertical but as soon as thin line has been produced, a straight tail is pulled that extends further to the right than the top. The wedge shape is narrower than for n.

x x

The success of x is largely determined by the slope of the first stroke. This is more vertical than might be imagined to produce a letter that looks compressed and sloping.

x

Experiment with different ways of adding the second diagonal.

z should be fairly narrow and written freely.

z

o, e, c and s are narrow letters. Some people

find it easier to construct o and e in two halves.

O may be slightly wider towards the top.

To make e in one stroke it should be started with the left corner of the nib half way between the guide lines.

The front edge of s aligns with a slope line and both top and bottom flattened. When beginning, make no part of s point uphill.

Flatten the top

Although this alphabet has had my personal touches and preferences added, I gratefully acknowledge the advice received from Tom Gourdie and Barbara Nichol. Though many flourishes have been developed from those of early manuscripts, or purely by experimentation, some have been influenced by other modern scribes, and I acknowledge the exciting variations of Ann Hechle and Ieuan Rees that have acted as a stimulus.

Some alternative letter shapes are :‑

94

For fast Italic handwriting, letter shapes need to be kept simple. The following changes to letters can add a little further elegance to both handwriting and more formal uses, but do take longer to construct.

A tick stroke on ascenders

A diagonal line drawn first, then curve back to start the vertical (exaggerated)

Start the ascender like starting an a

Pull the top stroke and finish with a comma

Push or pull a curved termination

or curve back, slide upwards

Note the bar formation

Ink drawn from a pulled stroke with the nib corner (tops)

OR The pen twisted on to its corner whilst finishing the last portion of the stroke (bar on f and t's.)

or

In the state of Queensland ...

abcdefg

hijklmno

pqrstuv

wxyz

For formal use,
the exit strokes on
letters are reduced.
The slope may be
decreased, and the
starting and finish-
ing touches to strokes
added.

All strokes on these
letters were pulled.

1234567890

Into the Spring Fields by
Emperor Koko. Scribe: Vi
Wilson, 1987. Gouache on
vellum. 200mm × 168mm.

*On the Taboo Against Knowing
Who You Are* by Alan Watts.
Scribe: Margo Snape, Gouache
on paper marbled by the scribe.
600mm × 400mm approx.

Single section book to illustrate
the binding method described in
the text. Scribe and binder:
Peter E. Taylor, 1983. Gouache
on Canson Ingres paper.
240mm × 150mm.

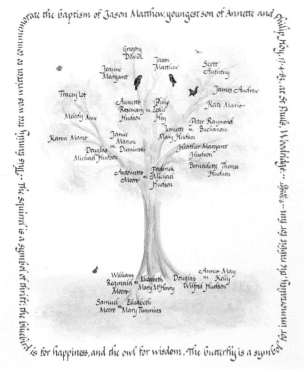

Family Tree to illustrate the painting method described in the text. Scribe: Peter E. Taylor from a idea by Lady Avril Watson-Stewart. Watercolour and gouache on Stonehenge paper. 500mm × 400mm.

Bifolium from *The Ark and Mrs. Goose* story and linocut by Pat Rowley, from a proof in the development of the book. Scribe: Vi Wilson, 1987. Chinese stick ink on T. H. Saunders hot press 150gsm paper, marbled endpapers also by the scribe. 375mm × 280mm.

After a few days, though, things began to go wrong.

One of the giraffes was disgustingly seasick, and not at all considerate to the other passengers.

Decorative initial and border pattern. Scribe: Barbara Nichol. Raised and burnished gold, gouache and watercolour. 100mm × 100mm.

Detail from an illumination.
Scribe: Kate Beukes. Transfer
gold on gum ammoniac
with gouache. 60mm × 80mm.

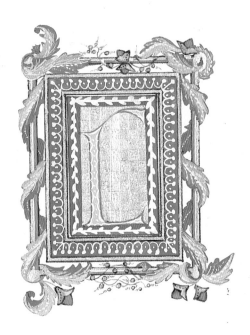

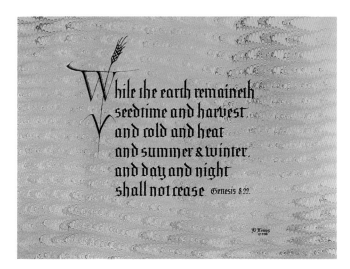

While the Earth Remaineth.
Scribe: Douglas Eising,
Marbler: Renata Eising.
420mm × 300mm
approx.

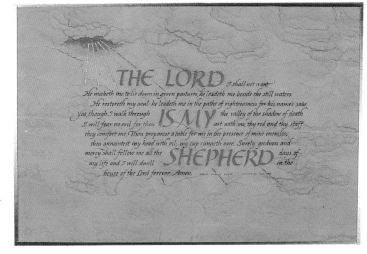

The Lord is My Shepherd.
Scribe: Vi Wilson, 1986.
Gouache on Japanese mulberry
paper. Gilding with gum
ammoniac and shell gold.
365mm × 240mm.

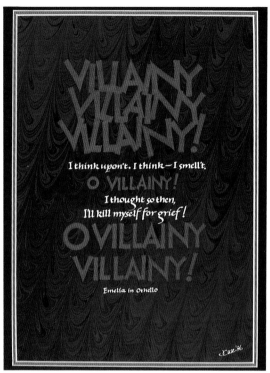

Villainy from *Othello* by William
Shakespeare. Scribe: Jon Case.
Gouache on marbled paper.
300mm × 220mm approx.

OUR FATHER WHICH
ART IN HEAVEN HALLOW-
ED BE THY NAME THY
KINGDOM COME THY
WILL BE DONE ON EARTH
AS IT IS IN HEAVEN GIVE
US THIS DAY OUR
DAILY BREAD AND
FORGIVE US OUR DEBTS
AS WE FORGIVE OUR
DEBTORS AND LEAD US
NOT INTO TEMPTATION
BUT DELIVER US FROM
EVIL FOR THINE IS THE
KINGDOM AND THE
POWER AND THE GLORY
FOREVER AMEN

The Lord's Prayer. Scribe: Jon
Case. 270mm × 230 mm approx.

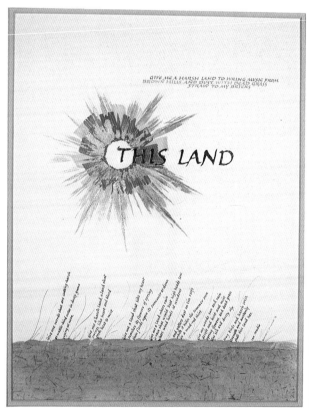

This Land by Ian Mudie.
Scribe: Vi Wilson, 1985.
Gouache, gum ammoniac gilding
and hard gilding on off-white
Stonehenge paper. Small overlay
of handmade paper.
325mm × 250mm.

The Last Rose of Summer by
Thomas Moore. Scribe: Barbara
Nichol, 1987. Painting in
watercolour and gouache.
200mm × 140mm.

Rain. Scribe: Dave Wood,
Ingres paper with gouache
applied with wood veneer.

East Wind by Hone Tuwhare.
Scribe: Dave Wood, 1986. Resist,
airbrush and gouache on Ingres
paper.

My Flight by Ghazels.
Scribe: Dave Wood. Airbrush
and knife on Arches paper.

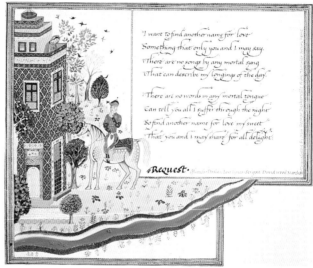

Request, translated by
Mrs G. Baskerville from Henri
Ferté. Scribe: Dave Wood, 1985.
Gouache and traditional gilding
on vellum.

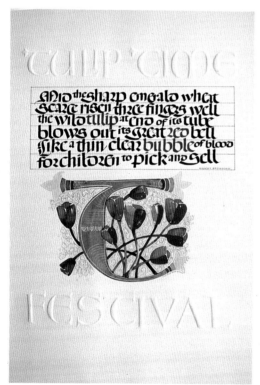

Tulip Time Festival by Robert
Browning. Scribe: Dave Wood.
Gouache on embossed Arches
paper.

Spring by Algernon C. Swinburne. Scribe: Dave Wood, 1986. Gouache on embossed Arches paper.

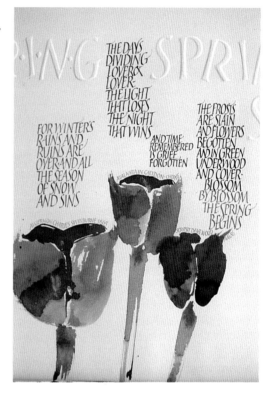

Moko by Hone Tuwhare. Scribe: Dave Wood. Gouache and gold paint on embossed Ingres paper.

Moko by Hone Tuwhare. Scribe: Dave Wood. Gouache on embossed Arches paper.

Rain. Scribe: Dave Wood. Steel nibs and wooden sticks with ink on laid Arches paper.

The Crystal Pyramid by W. S. Hughes. Scribe: Dave Wood. Airbrush and gouache on Ingres paper.

Song by Hone Tuwhare. Scribe: Dave Wood, 1987. Gouache on Ingres paper.

JOINING·LETTERS·

elegance

It is not essential to join letters. Letters may be well spaced to form words of solid appearance. Exit strokes may touch the next letter, but the aim is more in placing the letters so that the optical space between letters is equal to the area enclosed by u's and n's. This individual placement of letters is the only technique possible for formal Italic where the letters are compressed, but can be used for any writing if desired. The text of this book was mainly written in this way.

Though constructed separately, letters may be joined together by means of longer exit strokes to give the appearance of running writing.

1. Joins from i shaped exits to tick-shaped starts is by means of v shapes, the diagonal being pushed slightly vertically towards its termination. This termination is then covered as the next letter starts. Similarly, letters with tall ascenders may overlap and be dropped on to this type of exit stroke termination :—

ip il oil ail nip tube dull

97

2· From i shaped exits to curves, start by taking the exit stroke to about 3/4 of the 'x' height, keeping it straight, and making the curved letter blend so that a short area of the curve at its thinnest point matches on to the exit stroke:~

ic ag ue

Similarly from c and e :~ co ee

ice lag cage deed

It is best to keep to these simple joins initially, wherever it feels comfortable and natural; there will be times when the hand needs to be moved on the paper, and letters may remain unjoined at these places :~

When experience has been gained the hand will tend to be moved

reed

Hand was moved here

more when letters are dropped on to exit strokes, or as cross-strokes are made on t or f, or after a b, g, j, p, q, s or y .

3. There are many good books already on Italic hand-writing. Those by Tom Gourdie, Irene Wellington & Barbara Nichol are recommended. These provide many more examples and exercises than are possible here.

Joins in handwriting help with speed and fluid writing, but are generally kept to those previously described for any work where a degree of formality is required. Extra possible handwriting joins include:

a. Joins to n, m, and r, from letters with diagonal exit strokes, must move into a rounded entry to these letters, for example—

ir um ar

summer

Practice

mm

the rhythm

6. Those letters with horizontal terminations can lead straight on to vertical strokes, or extended to the start of curves, for example—

fire re

ri fu rc fa

from

99

t may join from the bar or the exit stroke

tu or *tu*

If e is constructed in two strokes

er ei ee are possible

either

c. Very slightly curved horizontal ligatures can join letters
that terminate on the top guide line with those that
start there. For example :-

wy oov vr

would

d. As confidence is gained exit strokes from the bottom
will be pushed to the top of some ascenders, with
the down stroke covering this top portion

As stated, joins never
have to be made and *ub* also *rt*
before an ascender is a good place to move the hand
or the paper. Some people never join particular pairs of

letters, but that is not 'wrong'. Similarly wordscan be broken in different places :–

nimble nimble nimble

After the break the next letter need not join on to the previous one in the normal way.

Some useful words to practice letter shapes, spacing and joins are—

little advance cover the top half of each word to check the lower apices of letters ...

medium infant very

letter fracture distinct

rite anguish Some letters were dropped on to v shaped exit strokes whilst others of the same shape were completed without the pen leaving the paper. With experience, diagonal exit strokes to curves will also be constructed at times :–

ed ng is

C·A·P·I·T·A·L·S   For writing complete words in capitals, a simple alphabet is preferred, based on Roman capitals with minimal additions. All capitals have to relate to the nature and finishing strokes of the minuscules used. The flourished or swash versions, for special occasions, still need restraint, with great pen control and precise movements and terminations. Unless enlarged greatly for special decorative purposes, it is best to keep them about 6½ nib widths high.

ABCDEFGHI
JKLMN NOP
QRSTUVWX

B D   The serifs of some   YZ   V W N

letters were reduced with a shallower pen angle.

The alphabet on the previous page is designed for very formal purposes. That drawn below, simply, is also able to be used when words need to be written completely in capitals, or for use within a text.

ABCDEF

GGHIJ

KLCMNN

OPQQ

RSTUVW

X

YYZ

K K K M
L N H
L e
L p P
q.4053 p P
P U
R Th V
W V
X X Y
Y
Z

b p p
k

F·L·O·U·R·I·S·H·E·S

A study of facsimiles or photographs
of the work of Renaissance writing
masters provide a good starting
point for the study of flourishes. They teach us that they
must be highly controlled
and in scale with the letter
sizes. Simple examples shou
ld be selected to start with ~
but make ascenders and descend
ers very large, about five times
the 'x' height, to give plenty of room.

·· REMEMBER ··
Bold cross-overs

Tiny white
spaces formed. Too many
lines meet in one place.

Many of the best flourishes get adapted from the pen movements made in ancient manuscripts :-

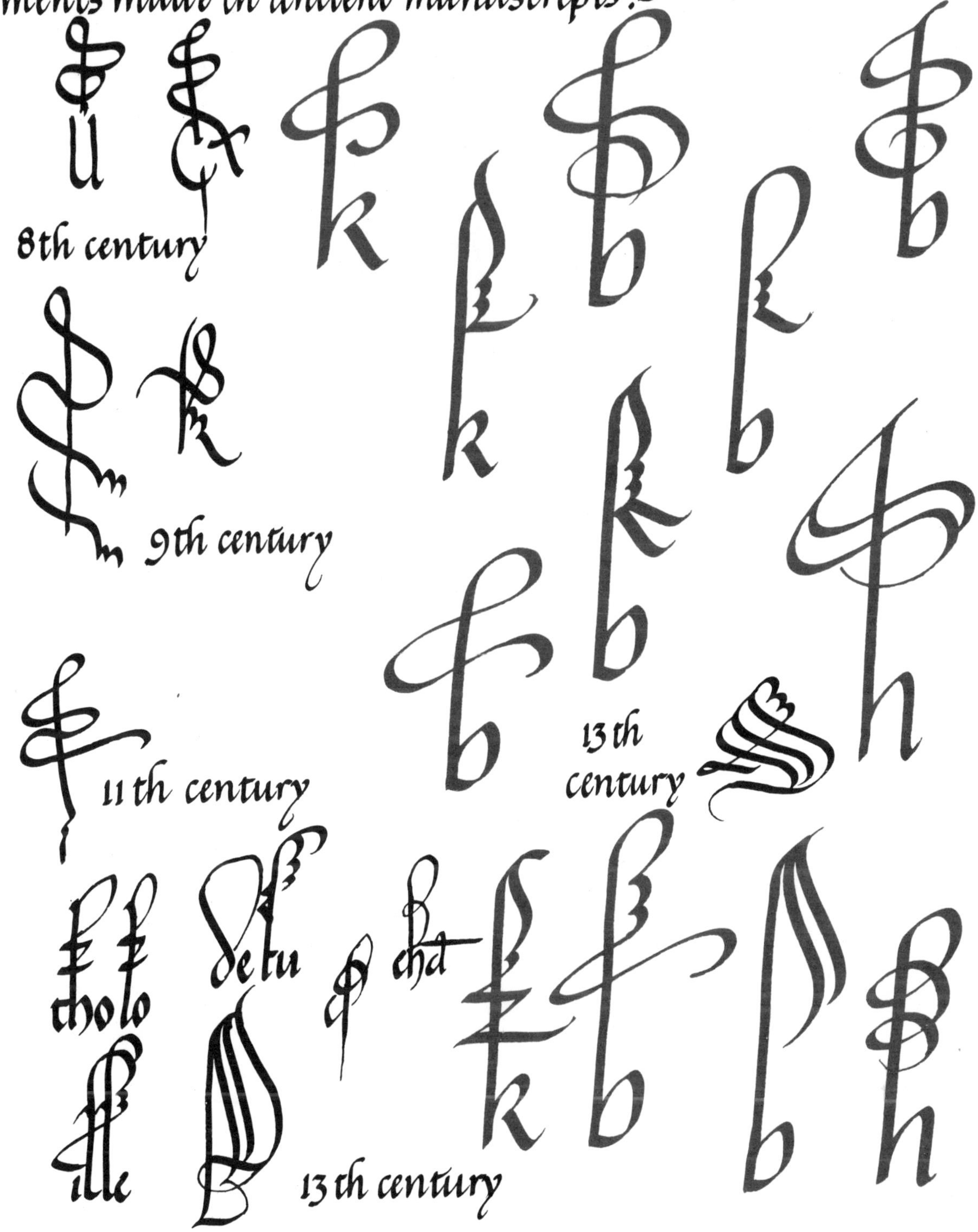

8th century

9th century

11th century

13th century

13th century

105

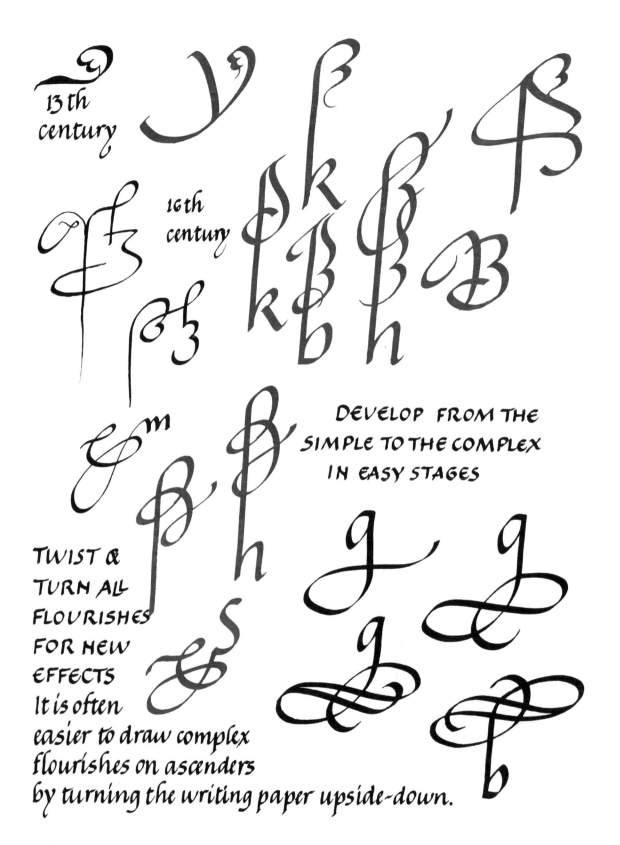

13th
century

16th
century

DEVELOP FROM THE
SIMPLE TO THE COMPLEX
IN EASY STAGES

TWIST &
TURN ALL
FLOURISHES
FOR NEW
EFFECTS
It is often
easier to draw complex
flourishes on ascenders
by turning the writing paper upside-down.

106

Try to copy versions that you like by tracing the pattern in mid air many times to commit it to memory before attempting it large on spare paper. The pen should move at a steady, constant speed. Then experiment with your own.

Decorations

Barry & Sue Brown invite you to a dinner to celebrate

the·twenty·first·birthday·of·Ann

on Sat. 23rd May 1987· at 7 pm· at 12, Park St. Ascot·1·May· R.S.V.P. 357.1112

As with all scripts, each calligrapher has their own preferences – in this case slope, degree of angularity and weight may be varied. This decision is made at least in part by the nature of the text to be written. Similarly, though the space between lines is usually about 1½ times the 'x' height of letters, this may be decreased or occasionally increased.

One way of increasing the angularity is to draw arch shapes with the left corner of the pen nib, and reapply the complete edge at the apex. Exit strokes and the bowls of a, d, g, q, and u and y, are also drawn with the corner.

abcdefg

hijklm

ɲ la nopqrs

h tuvwxyz

ɲ m The alternative terminations for h, n, and m.

ABCDEFGHIJK LMNOPQR STUVWXYZ

a·b·c·d·e·f·g·h·i·j·k·l·m·n·o·p·q·r·s·t·u·v·w·x·y·z·1·2·3·4·5·6·7·8·9·0·&·

Formal Scripts
and small spaces
create
in moderation
impact

& The Renaissance writing
manuals had wide spacing
between the lines and this
is useful for poems

The freely flowing cursive
can reflect the nature of poetry

angle
angle
angle

abc
xyz

All italic
varieties have
rhythm

im
pa
ct

create impact
flourishes
size
weight
line
spacing
colour
variation
create impact
create impact

a·b·c·d·e·f·g·h·i·j·k·l·m·n·o·p·q·r·s·t·u·v·w·x·y·z

8·· UNCIAL·
·and·half uncial·

Much of the earliest writing in Roman times was a copy of the letters that were carved in stone However, by the 4th century the characteristics of the square-ended nib were being exploited to write quickly on vellum, and some letter shapes were rounded to form the alphabet we recognise as uncial. This characteristic round-ness was maintained as some letters were added in a still quicker way to the essentialy 'capital' early uncial alpha-bet. The mixture is known as Roman Half-uncials.

these examples are about actual size

ROMAN UNCIAL OF THE FIFTH CENTURY

Insular half-

SIxth cent

uncials were

Roman

written in the

BRItish Isles

With the development of Christian centres in 6th cent
Ireland, Scotland and England, texts from Roman miss-
ionaries had to be copied. Scriptoria were set up, and books
were lent from one to another. Scribes trained in one
monastery may have moved to others. The Book of Kells,
from Ireland is, perhaps, the most famous example of
Insular Half-uncials, where most letter forms are of a
minuscule nature. They are based on wide, rounded letter
forms, with an almost constant pen angle close to horizontal, with joins between many letters.

The Book of Kells fame is due in particular, however, to
its wealth of beautiful, intricate, decorated pages. The
Lichfield Gospels share great similarities in written letter
forms. There are many other beautiful Celtic manuscripts;
for example, the Lindisfarne Gospels and the Book of
Durrow. The shared features in scripts and decorations
would seem to support the idea of a fair degree of travel
between monastic communities.

The Half-uncial script provided for copying is a simp-
lified version, whilst a more
original script is also given
for study. Suitable decorative
capitals and borders are described
in later chapters. The originals,
if possible, or photographs of them,
should be examined.

Many letters are built by the centre of the nib following part of a circle. In learning the script it is suggested that circles are drawn with a compass as a guide when building the letters.

Position yourself and the paper so that the pen will make its thinnest marks along the horizontal guide lines.

Practice thick and thin lines at right angles, and pull curved strokes in both directions, keeping the pen angle constant.

Whatever the size of nib used, writing lines should be the height of four times the nib width.

Most letters are based on the shapes of o, i, and n. Originally g was a totally different shape and k and w were not used.

Keep the centre of the nib on the line.

Most scribes start with the serif, though it can be completed last.

A dot may be added.

1   alternative   ii

He who knows not & knows not
that he knows not is a fool ~ Shun him
He who knows not & knows that
he knows not, is a child ~ Teach him
He who knows & knows not that
he knows, is asleep ~ Awaken him
He who knows, & knows that
he knows, is wise ~ Follow him

A Persian Saying. Scribe: Peter
E. Taylor, 1987. Ink over etching
The Seer by Brigid Marlin.
300mm × 230mm.

The Song of Love by Rainer M.
Rilke. Scribe: Vi Wilson, 1986.
Gilding with gum ammoniac on
J. Barcham Green handmade
paper.

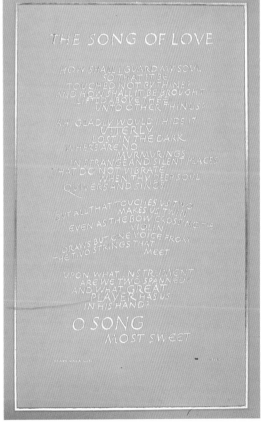

THE SONG OF LOVE

HOW SHALL I GUARD MY SOUL
SO THAT IT BE
TOUCHED NOT BY THINE?
AND HOW SHALL IT BE BROUGHT
LIFTED ABOVE THEE
UNTO OTHER THINGS?
AH, GLADLY WOULD I HIDE IT
UTTERLY
LOST IN THE DARK
WHERE ARE NO
MURMURINGS
IN STRANGE AND SILENT PLACES
THAT DO NOT VIBRATE
WHEN THY DEEP SOUL
QUIVERS AND SINGS

BUT ALL THAT TOUCHES US TWO
MAKES US TWIN
EVEN AS THE BOW CROSSING THE
VIOLIN
DRAWS BUT ONE VOICE FROM
THE TWO STRINGS THAT
MEET

UPON WHAT INSTRUMENT
ARE WE TWO SPANNED
AND WHAT GREAT
PLAYER HAS US
IN HIS HAND?

O SONG
MOST SWEET

The Seven Deadly Sins.
Scribe: James Corless,
1985. Inks.

An Invitation. Scribe: Margo Snape, 1985.

Menu Cover. Scribe: Barbara Nichol, 1987.

Poem by Vita Endelmanis.
Scribe: Barbara Nichol. Ink and
gouache on paper marbled by
the scribe. 300mm × 180mm
approx.

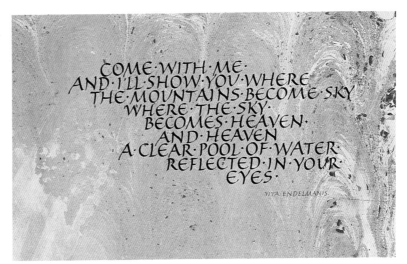

COME·WITH·ME·
AND·I'LL·SHOW·YOU·WHERE·
THE·MOUNTAINS·BECOME·SKY·
WHERE·THE·SKY·
BECOMES·HEAVEN·
AND·HEAVEN·
A·CLEAR·POOL·OF·WATER·
REFLECTED·IN·YOUR·
EYES·

VITA·ENDELMANIS

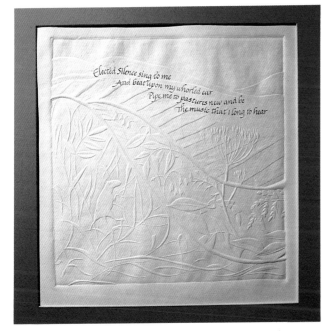

Elected Silence sing to me
And beat upon my whorled ear
Pipe me to pastures new and be
The music that I long to hear

Elected Silence by G. M.
Hopkins. Scribe: Peter E. Taylor,
1987. Gouache on Royal
Cornwall paper embossed by the
scribe. 320mm × 320mm.

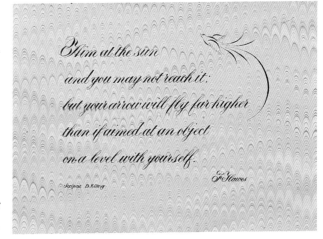

Aim at the sun
and you may not reach it:
but your arrow will fly far higher
than if aimed at an object
on a level with yourself.

Scripsit D. Eising

F. Hawes

Quotation from F. Hawes.
Scribe: Douglas Eising. Paper
marbling by Renata Eising.
300mm × 180mm.

This Land by Ian Mudie.
Scribe: Vi Wilson, 1986. 'Wet-in-wet' water colours and inks.
365mm × 265mm.

Give me a land that like my heart
scorches its flowers of spring
then floods upon its summer ardour.

Give me a land where rain
is rain that would beat high heads low
and patters dust on tin roofs

Where wind howls at the windows
while it hides the summer sun
in a mud-red shirt.

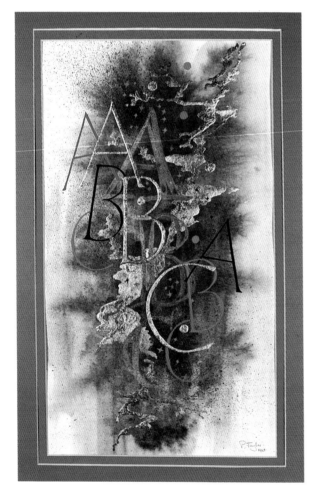

In the Beginning. Scribe: Peter E. Taylor.
Gilding on textured gum ammoniac,
with gouache. 400mm × 240mm.

Design for a cover. Scribe: Margo
Snape.

Poem by Lu Yu. Scribe: Don
Hatcher. Inks.
350mm × 250mm.

The Queensland Coat of Arms.
Scribe: Peter E. Taylor, 1982.
Gouache, with gilding on gum
ammoniac, on vellum. 100mm ×
100mm.

Poem. Scribe: Barbara Nichol.
Gouache on handmade paper.
300mm × 180mm.

Details from the Coat of Arms.

AX · AT · FIDELIS · :·

Details from the Coat of Arms.

Greetings from Ethna Gallagher.
Scribe: Ethna Gallagher, 1983.
Ink and gouache on paper.
650mm × 460mm.

Promotion for Donald Jackson
tour. Scribe: Ethna Gallagher,
1984.

Promotion for own classes.
Scribe: Ethna Gallagher, 1982.

Ned Kelly. Scribe: Rodney Saulwick. Ink, gouache, crayon and marker pens on Ingres paper with wood, quill, and a mixture of steel nibs. 365mm × 300mm.

Edward Kelly was born at Kilmore Victoria in 1885, and was hanged at Melbourne Gaol, 11th November 1880. Concluding the service Sir Redmond Barry said: "May the Lord have mercy on your soul." "Yes, said Kelly, I will meet you there." Two weeks later, Sir Redmond died.

Alphabet. Scribe: Margo Snape, 1985. 220mm × 160mm.

The left side of the vertical touches the circle. When the centre of the nib reaches the circle, the curves are formed, as for part of an o. n has a similar construction, but upside down.

circles overlap by one nib width

are other constructions

The base extends past the top, which is pulled slightly inwards from the circle.

or

e has the same basic construction as c.

However far the base extends past the top right edge, the base must overlap the left side of the top by the same amount. The area enclosed by the base is greater than that inside the top.

Note the different serif position for letter r.

r and **R**

Note the alternative joining order and slope (also w and y).

Note the pen angle changes.

Note the pen angle changes on x & z to produce a thinner diagonal on x and thicken the horizontals of z.

Z or Z or Z
Z
Z

After some confidence and speed has been achieved the structure of n, h, w & y may be varied. Possible alternatives are

nhwyy

When writing words it is probably best to leave joining strokes until the complete word has been written:—

letter

letter

Through dangly woods
the aimless doze
A-dripping and
 a-dribbling goes:
Whilst in the groves
 of dragon fungus,
lives the mysterious
 Chickamungus.

More ideas for the decoration
of capitals are provided in a later
chapter.

hijklmmn
nopqrst

with the nib corner

vwuxyʒƷ

For words written all in capitals
the straight line versions from the
Book of Kells or Lindisfarne Gospels could be used.

ABCD EFHIJL MNO

RSTUVX

It will be left to the
reader to design the
missing letters.

Arabic numerals were not in use at this time. Experiment!

1234567890

117

Each text or calligrapher's work studied will provide a different version of Celtic scripts.

A study of the more original letter designs below will provide some features that may be added as a personal style is developed. It will be noticed in the elementary alphabet, a tendency to slope the pen angle about 5-10 degrees, and for joining letters, to pull the bottoms a little to the right. This latter feature can also be seen in the Book of Kells. Strokes terminating vertically were thickened at the lower end, probably by increased pressure. For an authentic look, therefore, the feet of letters can have an extra stroke added. Spaces between words were smaller than a letter n.

The spacing between lines was about 8 nib widths

twisted pen

The thin joining strokes suggest some may have been drawn with the nib corner as part of an exit stroke, with the next letter covering the end.

The Insular manuscripts show the development of Half-uncials between the 6th and 10th centuries, with the Book of Kells being written in the late 8th or early 9th century.

Another type of uncial was also written in the 7th & 8th centuries in other centres, being of a majescule nature, constructed with many pen twists, angle changes & use of the corner of the nib. Some experience is therefore needed before this alphabet is attempted — and even the early scribes did not produce perfect letter shapes. Originally it was written about 3·5mm (3/16 in) high and difficulty with serif shapes was not noticeable when read normally. For 20th century use it can be mixed with other scripts, and provides a good contrast. When learning, an Automatic pen is recommended.

Rough of a message, to explore the mixing of scripts.

THE ❖ UNIVERSITY ❖ OF ❖

THE COUNCIL STAFF AND STUDENTS SEND THEIR WARMEST CONGRATULATIONS AND GREETINGS TO

In your time you have overcome many problems and developed a reputation ...

A AB C D E
F G C h I J K L
M N O P Q
R S T U
V W X Y Z

These strokes are drawn
with the left corner of
the nib only.

change pen angle to make ∠ and ∨

A B M

120

Slight change of pen angle

When the pen reaches this position, raise the right side of the nib slowly, keeping the left hand corner in motion on the paper, following the dots.

Faster lift →

More rapid raising of the right-hand side results in the < shape used in E,F,L and Z

FOR ALL THESE PEN TWEAKS, A FAIRLY FULL PEN IS NEEDED

Don't overdo the Dracula effect — no more than this.

For the top of T and Z, the left corner is raised whilst the right corner traces the curve downwards

Flat pen angle

Slow lift of right hand nib edge.
Path of left nib corner.

Pen angle

•Use the nib corner only.

•Trace this path with the right nib corner. Start lifting the left hand edge immediately, but slowly.

•Raise the right corner slowly whilst the left moves

•Right nib corner follows dots →

whilst lifting left side.

•Lift right nib corner slowly from here

•Fill in any white space with the nib corner

121

The following versions retain some features of the original, but have had the pen tweaks removed for serifs.

ΛΛBCDEFGhIJKL
MHOPQRSTUVI
ωXYZ

ABCDEFGhIJKKL
MHOPQRSCTTUV
ωXYZ

9··Some·Modern·Variations·

These alphabets have been selected and separated
to show how letter shapes may be developed, but
still retain the influences of the purer scripts of the past.

ROMAN

R Foundational

R

Italic

R Copperplate

R UNCIAL

Part of a letter-head
design for a glazier.

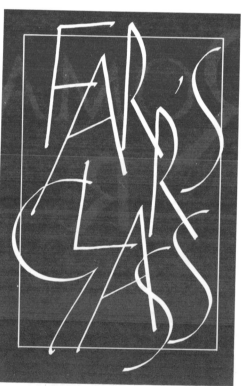

124

Both of these alphabets have strong 'Roman capital' overtones. They are both written fairly quickly. The previous example features a large height to nib width ratio. The nib width may be changed for some letters. This would enhance the uneven feel generated by the mixture of compressed and wide letter shapes.

This hand mixes well with Italic, and can be used when words are to be written in capitals, as well as for single capitals. They can be written the same size as the 'x' height of the italic minuscules – about 5 nib widths.

$A \cdot B \cdot C \cdot D \cdot E \cdot F \cdot G \cdot H$

$I \cdot J \cdot K \cdot L \cdot M \cdot N \cdot O \cdot P$

$Q \cdot R \cdot S \cdot T \cdot U \cdot V \cdot W$

$X \cdot Y \cdot Z$

THE PEN IS MIGHTIER THAN THE SWORD

By compression and changing the letter height to nib width ratio the script has a new feel to it. Its close relationship with the previous alphabet ensures harmony when used together.

Address for an envelope

JOHN·WILLIAMS
ARBUTUS PICTURE
FRAMING 176, Bray Rd.
Launton
Q·U·E·E·N·S·L·A·N·D

126

ANYONE·WHO· ISN'T·CONFUSED· DOESN'T·REALLY· UNDERSTAND· WHAT·IS·GOING·ON

A whole book could be written on Uncial variations.

This freely written saying shows many letters of Uncial origin, though with serifs reduced, and written with a pen angle at about 45 degrees.

A single thickness line retains much of the Uncial feeling when

MEN HELP EACH OTHER BY THEIR JOY

NOT THEIR SORROW

letter shapes reflect their ancient origin. Retaining the heavy serifs of the original forms, but compressing the letters and using a steepened pen angle, can lead to experiments in other directions:—

Ah, fill the Cup: what boots it to repeat
How time is slipping underneath our feet:
Unborn tomorrow and dead Yesterday,
Why fret about them if today be sweet?

127

10 ·· VERSALS ·

VERSAL letters are a form of capital based strictly on Roman Capitals for proportions, but with their vertical strokes 'waisted', and curved portions slightly exaggerated on the outside and flattened on the inside. The degree of exaggeration of these changes of shape will depend on the script they are to be used with.

D o D Heavy letters are suited to dense Gothic scripts, whilst letters closer to the proportions of the carved Roman shapes will look better en masse, or with lighter weight alphabets.

Versal letters are used for highly ornate and decorated initials, and this is covered in the chapter on Decorative Capitals. However they can be used with many writing styles and all versions are constructed according to the principles as follows ~

128

Straight strokes are only just off parallel.

Serifs are very thin and hollowed and added last of all.

Where additions are made to a vertical, the vertical is more hollowed on the outside than on the inside.

The inside of a curve is drawn first and flattened, then the outside is blended in.

When a letter consists of straight and curved elements, a) Construct the vertical first. b) continue the vertical stroke to produce the curved end portion. c) construct and complete the rounded portion, d) Add the serifs last. The thickness of the curved section in proportion to the upright will ultimately be determined by eye. However it will be approximately the width of the part shown.

In diagonal elements of letters, the serif is constructed with more thickness added to the outside of the stroke than the inside.

Essentially Versals are drawn letters, and a narrower nib than that used for writing is selected. Pen angles can be changed from horizontal for verticals, curves and diagonal strokes,

to horizontal for horizontal elements of letters, and vertical
serif strokes. Letters can then then be left hollow, or filled in,
or decorated. Instead of using a pen, letters can also be drawn,
then painted with a brush.

ABCDEFGHIJ
KLMNOPQR
STUVWXYZ

This alphabet was very freely drawn. The letters may be
made more formal, if so desired, or exaggerated further.

For the capital at the start of verses, Versals
in alternate colours, perhaps blue and red,

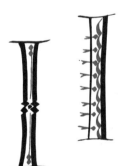

In·The·Be
God created
earth.

The Decorative Capitals
chapter gives more ideas
for additions to letters

make a simple addition to a poem. Titles completely written in Versals can be very effective. There are a few basic alternative designs ~

A·D·E·H
M·N·N
S·T·U·W

Historic examples by well practised professional scribes have a particular freshness, and photographs and originals should be studied. Their use of colour, ingenious, complex interweaving, positioning and decoration, can still teach us much as we explore the possibilities for their use in our own designs.

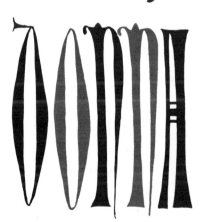

It is a good idea to keep a sketch book

ABCDEF GHIJKLM NOPQRS TUVW XYZ

This alphabet has been constructed for the heavier appearance needed for capitals for Gothic styles, and is suitable for many decorative treatments.

Simple Versals may be used for formal headings to charters and other documents, or with subtle colour changes in massed writing and in many other ways. They are not easy to construct, but practice in the building of letters in this way will enable modern letter shapes, built from more than one pen stroke, to be designed ~

ABCDEFGHIJKLM
NOPQRSTUVWXYZ

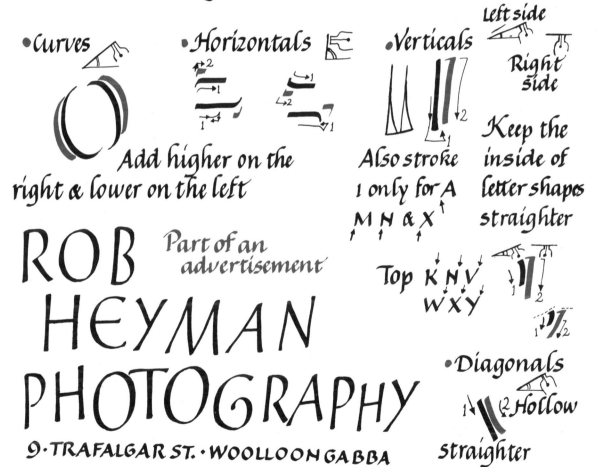

•Curves

Add higher on the right & lower on the left

•Horizontals

•Verticals

Also stroke 1 only for A M N & X

Left side

Right side

Keep the inside of letter shapes straighter

Top K N V W X Y

•Diagonals

Hollow straighter

ROB HEYMAN PHOTOGRAPHY

Part of an advertisement

9·TRAFALGAR ST.·WOOLLOONGABBA
Q·4102·(07) 834 6061

11. Copperplate

With the development and more widespread use of printing in the 16th century, many scribes turned to teaching, and published their individual exemplars & manuals. The plates of copper used in the printing were engraved with a dexterity that allowed for very gentle changes of line thickness, with many thin line flourishes. The plate was turned in many directions. As with the woodblock printing method for the 'Operina' and other Italic hands, very tight curves were hard to cut and the writing masters exploited the characteristics of the copperplate printing method. They designed new alphabets and increasingly more complex decorations to win acclaim. With a sharpened quill that could produce thick strokes with increased pressure, and the finest of thin lines when no pressure was applied, the alphabets and texts could be copied without much lifting of the pen between letters or strokes. Its speedy execution enhanced its popularity, and square-cut pens died out of use and were not manufactured when steel nibs were first made.

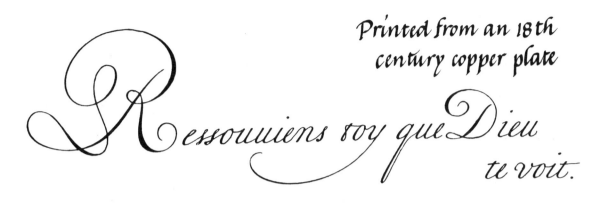

Printed from an 18th century copper plate

Ressouuiens toy que Dieu te voit.

The writing copy books continued to be published through the 18th century by writing masters, and facsimiles or photographs of pages from them should be examined. 'The Universal Penman', originally published between 1733 and 1741 is probably the most readily available in facsimile form (Dover 1941). The letter forms are written with a constant pen hold, but many of the ornaments and flourishes in most original books require the paper or arm to be turned, in their construction.

Here, the letter shapes are of a straightforward design, with no pen manipulation used. They were drawn, along with the practice words, by Heather Taylor and grateful thanks are given for this contribution.

The pointed and flexible nib used has to be in line with the steep slope angle of the script at all times. The William Mitchell Elbow oblique Copperplate nibs are recommended. The Gillott 404 is also a good nib for

55°

beginners for larger writing. This may be used in an angled pen holder, as may Hunt Imperial 101 nibs for smaller writing. After some experience has been gained, Gillott 303 and Hunt 99 or 22 nibs may be tried. As with all metal nibs, the grease on the surface needs to be removed prior to use, either with saliva, detergent or other solvent, or boiling water. The ink needs to be a little thicker than for other styles. Pelikan Fount India is preferred by many, but other varieties can be thickened by the addition of a few drops of gum arabic, or by allowing them to evaporate.

A piece of paper should be kept at the side of the work to test the pen on. After refilling, the pen should be able to produce hair thickness thin lines on upstrokes. Reservoirs are not made for copperplate nibs, but those made for William Mitchells Roundhand nibs will fit with a little bending.

a o The bowl of a is an ellipse. It is started almost vertically, about 2/3 rds up from the bottom guide line, with no pressure applied. The pressure is built up gradually after the top has been turned, and is released as soon as the return part of the stroke begins to turn right. There is no pressure at the bottom. It is best to lift the pen to add the next stroke which just skims the o shape. Pressure is applied before the pen moves, to make a square ended top. The press ure is taken off the nib as it moves around the curve. There is none on the bottom or on the upstroke, which is parallel to the down stroke. The width of the u shape is the same as the ellipse.

The lead-in stroke hesitates at half way, then forms a hair line loop. Pressure builds up after the top apex and the bottom has the shape of the a. To complete the letter a tiny inward loop is formed, with pressure to fill it in, then a curved exit stroke suitable for a smooth movement to the next letter of a word.

The c starts in the same position as an o shape. A dot is produced, with pressure, as a tight anti-clockwise circle, before the letter is formed with a slightly wider shape at the bottom.

d is constructed as an a, with a tall ascender. With a hesitation at the end of an entry stroke, a smooth movement is made across to the right to start the c stroke.

Other texts will provide a range of variants of f. It can be left square ended. The lower loop crosses about midway, in this example, whereas that of g crosses on the lower guideline. The pressure is released gradually at the end of the descender to be completely thin at the tip. The tail of g is narrower than for Italic or other styles described so far.

h h is made up from the start of b, with a square end on the bottom. The shape at the side of this is the reverse of the u shape to begin with, starting in the direction of the slope line. It need not touch the thick stroke if ink fills in the angle between the two elements.

i is a u shape which terminates midway *i* *j* between guidelines. j starts in a similar fashion with a g shaped tail.

k k starts in the same way as h.

l is the b shape without the tightened *l* loop at the end. The loop on the vertical of l starts at the top guide line for the x height.

m m and n are created with the reverse u shape, as for h, at the start. Pressure is built up *n* after the top point has been reached, whilst the curve is being produced. Note the position and direction of the second and third upstrokes.

Like the b, o continues from the joining of the *o* ellipse with a small anticlockwise movement, and some pressure, to form a dot inside, and a curved exit stroke.

The descender of p is started a small distance above

the top guide line for the 'x' height, and should
have both ends square.

The loop of q almost meets the descender
at the bottom guideline.

The dot for the letter r is formed to sit on
top of the guide line. It is easy to make this
letter too wide or too narrow.

The lead-in stroke extends above the guideline. The bowl of the letter starts on the top
line, with no pressure, and its front edge is almost vertical.

The top of t is ⅓rd the way between i and l, & the
bar can be put on, only on the right, at the same
level as the 'x' height. Some people prefer to cross
higher, right through, and make the top of the letter
halfway between i and l. Crossing t after the vertical has
dried somewhat maintains perfect corners at the joins.

Letter u starts with heavy pressure, which eases
off ⅓rd of the way from the bottom guide line. It
curves around to the right with no pressure. This stroke
is then repeated.

v is formed like the right-hand half of h,
with a b-type dot and exit.

w is a combination of u and v.

To maintain the impression of slope the
first stroke is almost vertical in the centre.

The second stroke has to pass through the centre.
  y is started like v, the pen moved, then the
completion of g added.
  z starts like the n stroke, but curves with
pressure added. A small fine loop on the lower
guideline is formed and a g shaped tail completes the
the stroke. The hairline, however, crosses just below the line.

Most capital letters have ellipses in their structure —

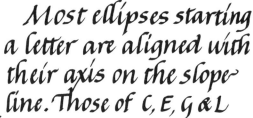

Most ellipses starting
a letter are aligned with
their axis on the slope-
line. Those of C, E, G & L
have their axes horizontal. They are started with no
pressure on the pen nib.
  The other feature that many letters have in common
is the stroke that would have been vertical in the Roman alphabet. This has to follow the angle of the slope-
line.   It gradually builds up in thickness, then
             moves into a generous but flattened curve
             with a small dot, made as a continuous
clockwise loop.
             The axis of A has to look as though it is on
             the slope line. The first stroke is angled a
             little more than the slopeline, the second more
vertical, with building pressure.

B Like Roman B's the lower bowl has a slightly larger area than the top one, and the front edge joining both curves is almost vertical. There are a large number of elliptical shapes in this letter.

C C comprises a number of elliptical parts too ~ one is horizontal, and two are on slopelines.

D looks narrow but seems to work best *D* that way.

The down stroke of F is completed *F* *E* first, then the top ellipse and horizontal.

I and J are made up in two parts.

G H I J K L The base of L may be drawn under the lower line of the 'x' height to keep area between letters looking more constant.

M Its hard to make M look on the correct slope with balanced angles. The letter is formed without the pen nib leaving the paper. The first part of the v stroke is thin at both ends and almost vertical.

As with M, the diagonal of N has no pressure *N* applied at each end.

O P Q R

S *T*

The loop created at the top of S moves fluidly into the upright. Experiments may be made with larger and deeper loops.

It is good to practice V with a slope line passing through the apex to get the angles of the strokes balanced. *V*

U

W *X* *Y* *Z*

1 2 3 4 5

6 7 8 9 0

Note that 0, 6 and 9 are thickened on both sides. Some prefer also to add extra strokes to the top of 5 to thicken it a little.

When writing words, as with other scripts, the aim is to make the spacing look optically even. The space between words is that of letter o. Words for the practice of joins are

begin *animal* *ginger* *home*

142

12 · · Other·Aspects·of·Design·

throughout this book illustrations have been
selected to give as wide a range of
ideas as possible, showing how different scripts can be used
together, using different sizes of writing in one text, and so
forth. Here some of these techniques are explained, and new
ones considered, hopefully to provide some tools for further experimentation, and the production of a personal style of work.
Some useful, practical tips are also included.

SHAPED·WRITING

Grantin·Fishing·Club
Private·Waters
Tickets·from·kiosk

A text may be written with line endings adjusted to make
a shape of a feature related to the text. The manipulation

of letters in a single word to make a shape is harder, but fun to try. Words can also be repeated to make up designs, and can be very effective in different colours.

Poems are often able to be written on curved lines, even as a circle or spiral. Corners on borders also need to be turned. Each part of the curve is considered part of circle. Letters are written with vertical strokes aligned with radii. The strokes within a letter remain

parallel, m, for example is aligned on its mid point.

Verses which appear to 'wind up' would move towards the centre of a spiral, but

If apples bloom in March, in vain for one you'll sarch. If apples bloom in April, then they'll be plentiful. If apples bloom in May, eatem night & day.

Plant four seeds
to a hole~
one for the rook
One for the crow
One to rot
And one to grow

an outward moving rough would determine the starting point.

Contrasting colour and writing size can produce texture, with darker colour overlapping paler, perhaps. Another idea is to use one colour only, but in tones and tints, by adding black and white.

COLOUR

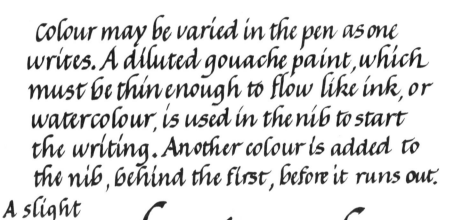

Colour may be varied in the pen as one writes. A diluted gouache paint, which must be thin enough to flow like ink, or watercolour, is used in the nib to start the writing. Another colour is added to the nib, behind the first, before it runs out.

A slight blending of colours results in a transition from one to another. Care must be taken not to over fill the nib & for subtle changes

Blend reds, orange & purple

145

many intermediate colours have to be premixed. Water may also be added for dark to pale effects.

The use of colour in capitals and borders is dealt with elsewhere. However, other letters may have gold or colour added to them. Multicoloured stained glass window effects are joyous for greetings cards, perhaps, whereas more simple colour schemes with one colour and a tint of that colour may be more appropriate for other work. The effectiveness of such a treatment

Stained glass

may be seen in the Book of Kells. Colours should not touch the letter or each other. Darker colours in larger spaces between letters that were not well spaced when written, can help in the general appearance of some texts

Large presentations & certificates usually benefit from one or two colours only being used, apart from black. Overall balance is needed and colour used at the top should usually be found at the bottom too, even if only as ribbon colour, or decorations in flourishes.

In less formal pieces, decorat

146

devices can give an extra binding force, with careful placement, but the text must still be the dominant element. These devices include small squares, snowflakes, crosses, circles and other geometric designs of related colour to part of the text.

For greetings cards and envelopes, the use of colour and decoration can be more flamboyant, though unity must still feature strongly in design considerations. Envelopes may be written in colours appropriate to the stamps which, if of low denomination, can be arranged in patterns, as can Air mail stickers. Calligraphic felt pens that are getting pale, are useful for background lettering or designs.

Colours may also be blended by adding a spot of colour to the wet ink or paint after each letter has been written.

PETER TAYLOR
57 · REMICK ST ·
STAFFORD HTS ·
QUEENSLAND
4053 ·

Brush pens made by Pentel and other manufacturers, come in many colours. A mixed handful can also

57 · Remick Street · Stafford Hts

PETER TAYLORS Q4053

CALLIGRAPHICS

be used for colourful backgrounds and spontaneous designs suitable for cards.

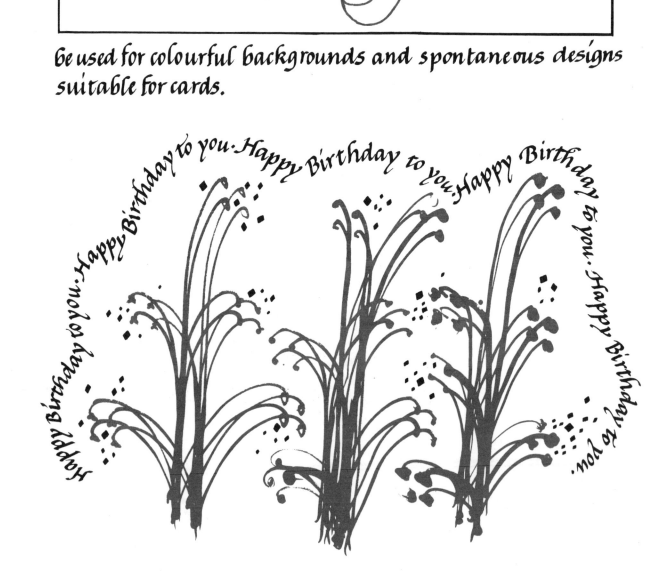

148

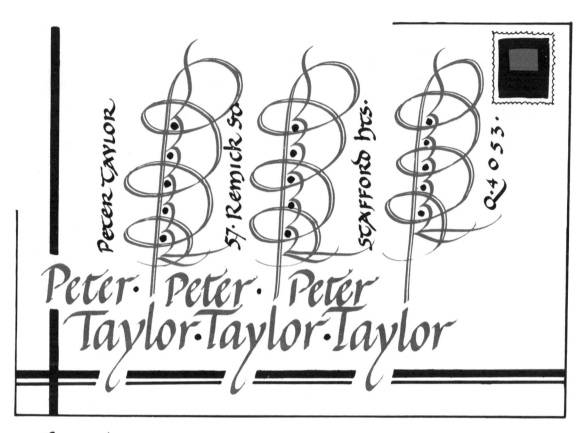

Peter · Peter · Peter
Taylor · Taylor · Taylor

The cutting of erasers to make repeatable design stamps provides a quick tool for envelope decoration and making

greetings cards. Gouache paint, ink, felt or brush pens can be used for printing. More than one print from a colour application will give a range of tones.

EMBOSSING

This process of forming paper into a raised design involves the cutting of letters or shapes into a material hard enough to maintain its edges, whilst a sheet of strong paper is pressed into the spaces.

Details may be carved into photographic or picture framers mount board, or thick 'grey board' as would be used for the hard covers of books. Damp paper can be placed over tissue on top of the carving, and an etching press used with care to mould the paper without crushing the design.

For more simple work a hard paper such as Fabriano 121 GF, 300 gsm, which can also be purchased as an Asco Canberra pad, can be cut for the template, or medium weight card. Leaf shapes, Christmas and other designs are very successful apart from letters, which may be written on the template material with a wide nib, or two pencils taped together. The inside area of the letter strokes is removed, retaining any parts of the spaces inside letters that become detatched. A sheet of thin paper has the cut out design glued to it in reverse, attaching areas needed to complete letters, and giving strength to thin areas. The paper on to which the design is embossed needs to be soft enough to be moulded, but have enough

strength not to tear as it is creased. It is placed, dry, over the reversed design, so that the paper can be pushed into the hollows of the template. This is most easily accomplished by placing the work against a window or a light box, and a 7mm (No.2) knitting needle used to press the paper against the inside edges of the cut-out shapes. Borders can be added in the same way. Recipes may be written around or inside embossings of fruit, for example, logos raised and poems written around related designs. Pastelle paper embosses well but is difficult to write on. Stonehenge is excellent, as is thick Conqueror paper.

RESISTS AND COLOUR REVERSAL

Writing with white ink or paint with an even density is extremely difficult, particularly with wide pens. A printer is able to reverse the colour so that black writing appears white, and what was white, print any colour.

An alternative is to write or paint with rubber masking

fluid, such as that manufactured by Winsor and Newton. When it is dry, paint or ink is brushed over all the area & then when that is dry, more masking fluid can be applied. By blending colours, toned letters or backgrounds can be produced when the rubber is peeled off, may be with aid of an eraser or a pin. Experimentation is needed with inks, papers and techniques, as it is easy to disturb underlayers of rubber when you write one on top of another, and erasing can smudge colours into each other.

ROUGH PAPERS

Freely drawn letters on rough paper can give an extra feeling of joy in their execution by the sparkle of the paper colour that remains where the nib did not touch. Usually one has to write fairly large, and bamboo or reed pens are excell~ent for this. Conté pastels are square sectioned and write well on ingres and laid papers.

STACKING Letters and lines of writing placed very close, touching or even overlapping, may be called 'stacked'. It is tempting to think that letters can be placed anyhow. Some guidelines, however, often help with perhaps three or four levels only being used on each line. It is easy,

WHAT YOU ARE IS GOD'S GIFT TO YOU · WHAT YOU MAKE OF YOURSELF IS YOUR GIFT TO GOD

too, to produce confusion. **GORY** is easily read GORY, or **LQVE** as LQ. Overlaps should be bold, and no joins or crossovers should produce large extra-thick areas, or tiny corners of white space. An even texture on the page is aimed for. If holes of white space seem unavoidable, these could be suitable places for a signature and a date.

MONOGRAMS

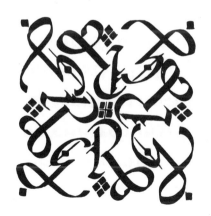

The intertwining or joining of letters to form mono-grams is a test of ingenuity. They can be used effectively as logos for corporate identity, or simply for notepaper and envelopes. Bookplates, too, can feature such devices, which may be used along with the person's name, as elements within a design, by repeating them as radii, or forming a square or other geometric construction. The original monogram is traced on to an overlay sheet, which is moved to explore ways of fitting them together.

PEN DRAWN DESIGNS

Pen drawings can be very effective as borders, inside capitals, for greetings cards, and as illustrations. One important consideration is the relative size of the nib width to the size of the drawing. Plant and animal drawings in particular need care that thick and thin lines come in appropriate places. This may be accomplished by twisting the paper and changing the pen angle several times in one drawing. A mixture of nib sizes can also be used, and the nib corner used to draw out the finest of lines from the wet ink or paint.

Jelly slice

CRUMB·CRUST~ ½ pkt. wheatmeal biscuits (crushed) · 2-3oz melted butter · · 1 tabsp. brown sugar · ½ teasp. cinnamon ·

Mix together and press into a slice tray. Refridgerate.

·TOPPINGS· Make up a red jelly and allow to cool.

· 1 400gm condensed milk · juice of 2 lemons · 2 teasp. gelatine disolved in ¾ cup of hot water (cool before use) ·

Combine and pour over crust and cool to set before adding jelly.

INVITATIONS

Standard format invitations are designed in the same way as any other piece of centred work. The centring technique is described in the earlier design chapter. However, the line spaces have to be carefully adjusted to allow for the folding of the paper.

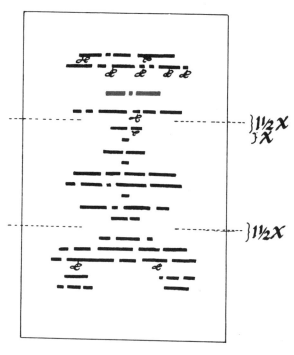

A sheet of paper the size of the finished item, is first folded to match the chosen envelope. When opened out, the writing lines are positioned so that the crease is halfway between lines of writing, and the space between these lines is half as large again to double the space between ordinary lines of writing. This is usually done for printing by writing it out with normal line spacing throughout, then cutting up the copy and repasting it on to a new sheet with the changed spacing.

A card template may be used for 'ruling' lines on envelopes.

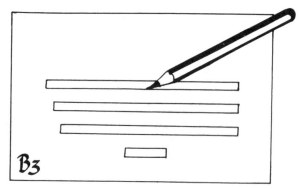

FILLING IN NAMES

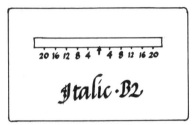

Italic · B2

If a large number of names have to be filled in and centred on invitations, place cards or certificates, a cut out card may be used to mark guidelines. It can also have marks on it to suggest where to start and finish names of particular lengths, e.g., typed ten letters (remembering to allow for spaces) or 5cm of type. This can be reasonably accurately determined from writing out about ten names in rough. If the starting strokes of capitals are simple, flourishes may be added later to balance the centring, or terminal strokes increased on the last letter if necessary.

157

Dear _____

You are invited

21st Birthday dinner at Terrace Railway Chevalier's June Milton Restaurant R.S.V.P. w9 on 16th to attend Paul's 7.30

Dear _____

You are invited
to attend
Vi's half
way to 70

Birthday Dinner

at Ardrossan Restaurant
33, Brookes St.·Bowen Hills
Sat. 6th Jan · at 7.30 p.m.

R·S·V·P·

Thank you for the invitation to your party. We look forward to being with you.

Dear
Pat at

Best wishes
Chris & Tony

Experiment!

13··Painting·

There are many ways in which paint can be used in conjunction with calligraphy. Backgrounds, decorations, heraldic crests and the letters themselves will be considered here. It is important to realise, however, that any additions must not detract from the readability of the text. The techniques described here are by no means exhaustive, and each calligrapher develops a very personal approach in both colours and media. A great deal of experimentation is therefore recommended.

BRUSHES Fine sable brushes are needed for much detailed work. Sizes 0 and 1 are particularly useful. They have to hold enough paint to make good lengths of line or cover a sufficient area, but must still come to a needle point. Larger sizes may be practical for watercolour wash techniques and filling in larger areas. Old brushes or cheaper ones are usually used for mixing paint and loading it into a pen.

PAINT Calligraphers should be aware of the permanence of the medium they use. Some colours are not as light fast as others, and this information is provided by the manufacturer. Others contain minerals that will react with sulphur in the air and change colour, or even react with the colour next to them. Inks, in particular are likely to fade after several years.

For those who wish to produce the type of work that will last for centuries and are concerned about the effects of acid in the paper they use on the paint colours, more specialist books should be consulted, e.g., 'The Calligrapher's Handbook' (Taplinger, 1986), and 'Painting for Calligraphers' by Marie Angel (Pelham Books, 1984). The following information should provide a sound basis for most workers.

For transparent effects water colours are preferred. Winsor & Newton make an excellent range in pans and tubes. The tubes of Artists' colours are the most convenient for mixing, particularly for large washes. Water is added to the desired degree of transparency.

The greatest opacity is produced from gouache colour. Winsor and Newton Designers' colours in tubes are a personal choice. They are diluted with water until they will just trickle around the mixing palette, for a good covering power over an area or for use in a pen. They can also be diluted to be watery and transparent like water colors, but lack a little of the sparkle of the real thing when used in this way.

160

Patterns may be used in many ways. Gouache can be used in some areas and contrasted with transparent watercolour in the same or a different hue. Areas or decorations in gold can enhance the overall effect.

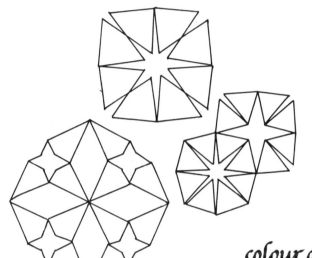

If large washes of colour are to be used, the paper may need to be stretched as for watercolour painting. After this has been done, writing may be more difficult. When dry it could be sprayed with a charcoal fixative, or gum sandarac dust applied by a dabbing action using the ground resin tied up in a small bag of fine cotton or similar fabric. If writing over a painted background, the surface to be written on is treated after painting, and all particles of the resin dusted off.

If the written area will be away from the paint it is probably best to sandarac the area for writing first, (avoiding the area to be painted), dust off all surplus, then write, then paint. In this way the paint colours and design may be adjusted to maintain the correct balance of the completed work. A stippled effect in painting — made up from many small strokes — can avoid the need for stretching paper, and vellum is less likely to distort too.

Apart from large painted washes, back-grounds may also be

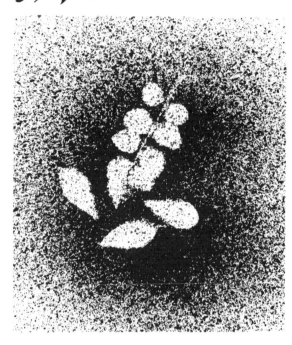

added with the stipple effect of paint in a sponge, or sprayed on with an air brush, atomiser or toothbrush (try this on scrap paper first to determine the size of the dots)

The background for the colour plate 'In the Beginning' was produced by pouring mixtures of Ultramarine Blue, Burnt Umber and Lamp Black on to wet paper. Just as the gloss was going from the wet paint, the letters were drawn with a brush that had been moistened and squeezed nearly dry.

MEDIA

Different effects will be obtained if paint is mixed with different media. A drop or two of egg yolk, separated from all membranes, as shown, mixed with Vermillion and a little water, gives the colour an extra 'lift' and was used in medieval times. It can be used with other colours too, but addition of gum water can also be tried. However, if too much is added the paint will crack. Apart from the extra brilliance they both give, they can be helpful where the colour may get brushed off in use. Glair is another possible addition to pigments. Egg white is beaten to a hard froth. A tablespoon of this is added to a tablespoon of water and left overnight. The liquid that settles out is glair. It is similarly mixed with the paint, with a little water added if necessary.

When drawing on vellum, hard pencils, about 2H, are

best. Smudges from soft pencils are hard to erase (try gum erasers or new bread). After the subject has been drawn, pale water colour (possibly an 'earth' colour such as an Umber) added over the lines. The pencil is then erased. A 2B pencil, sharpened to a neede point and used very lightly, is particularly useful on paper

The hair side of vellum is used most easily for painting and writing, and though it may be sanded and brought to a nap for writing, It is best left smooth for painting. It may be worthwhile, however, for work that will be framed, to explore the possibilities of painting on the underside of vellum, the flesh side, too. If thin enough, some effect will be seen through the skin.

COLOURS

The balance and selection of colours is very personal. They have to be considered not only on their own, but for their effects on other areas near them. They may make these look smaller or brighter than they would in isolation. My own palette is restricted to the following for most work—

Prussian Blue – occasionally used by itself, but more frequently used with yellow to make a good range of greens.

Ultramarine Blue – also blended with yellow to make green. A range of blues made using Ultramarine includes the addition of white or Cerulean Blue

Cerulean Blue ~ is also used to make pastel greens.

Cobalt Blue ~ is a good starting point for Heraldic and other blue mixtures, as well as for green.

Sky Blue ~ with a tiny touch of white, is brilliant on putty coloured parchment paper.

Permanent Blue ~ is used to make mauve and purple with Alizarin Crimson.

Lemon Yellow or Spectrum Yellow ~ used the most to make green. Other yellows used are Yellow Ochre and Aureolin.

Scarlet Lake or Flame Red ~ are used as a substitute for Vermillion, which is very expensive.

Alizarin Crimson ~ makes good pinks and purple, both with Permanent Blue and Ultramarine. Sometimes it will tend to separate with Ultramarine to give more blue around the edge. This can be attractive or a nuisance.

Raw and Burnt Umber ⎫ These may be blended with
Raw and Burnt Sienna ⎬ other colours & each other.

Zinc White ~ for tints

Permanent White or Titanium White ~ for lines over other colours and making other colours more dense for greater covering power. This last function is performed by Chinese White in watercolour.

Lamp Black

When first purchasing a limited range of colours, the best selection is probably—

Ultramarine Blue, Scarlet Lake, Alizarin Crimson, Permanent White, Lemon Yellow, and Burnt Umber.

On the finished painted page one looks for balance, harmony of colour and focal point, as in any picture. One must also be aware of maintaining margin proportions in books.

If plants or animals are included, scale is important, and detail must be observed. A sketch book is useful – drawing

from nature. In painting animals it is especially important that the strokes made by the brush are in the same direction that the hair or feathers grow on the actual creature concerned. There are many subtle changes on faces, and around shoulders and joints in limbs. There are also many changes of colour on one leaf, over the length of a stem, and certainly in fur and in each feather of birds. One way of portraying this is with an underpainting of thin washes, possibly adding slightly darker wet colour to the very wet underpaint so that the two colours blend in a way that suggests the curved nature of the subject. Pale watercolour can next be added in fine strokes, after the underpaint has dried, and darker layers gradually built up, perhaps with gouache. A tiny amount of pure black and pure white often provide the finishing touch. When painting fur the pressure on the brush is increased in the middle of each stroke.

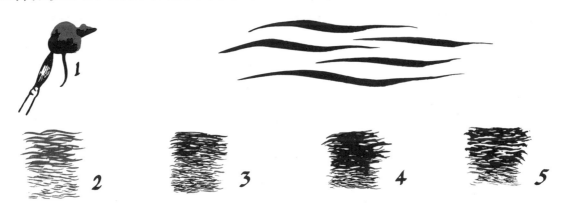

Similarly when painting leaves a yellowish underpainting wash may be laid down first. Grey washes may be added next, with modelling to show overall curvature & the raised or sunken nature of the veins. Fine strokes of blue greens are then built up over many layers, and white highlights added last. Simplified versions are also effective, however, especially when small ~

Small animals may only need modelling, though I usually try to add a few dark strokes along the back, around the back of the head, and where the limbs join the body. Feathers are suggested by small dabs of slightly darker paint than the background wash, and clear bands for the main wing flight feathers. Stylised leaves are based, in shape, upon living specimens, with transparent colour blended whilst wet. Overpainting may add darker tone to one edge, make one half darker than the other, or form more complex patterning.

Many will wish to add leaves and plants to intertwine capitals and form borders, but it should be noted that they start from a point and grow and branch in the same way that real plants do. Before the use of a fine brush is mastered to produce very thin lines, a crow quill or mapping nib should be used for fine stems and tendrils. It is very easy to get a muddy look with gouache paint, and a watery green is suggested for stems, and about four or five colours of green, in transparent watercolour for leaves. Similarly, outlining leaves is probably best left until experience has been gained, but one half of some leaves can be painted in a more bluish shade than the other half, to good effect.

Drops of water are placed next to the paint.

The water is stroked through the paint.

Excess paint is scraped from the brush.

For painting curves, outlines and most detail I hold a brush to form a T shape with my thumb. The paper is turned so that the brush can be lined up with the bristles pointing along the stroke. For curves, outlines and other long strokes the aim is to pull the brush smoothly along the whole length of the line, rather than using a dabbing action. Outlines are completed, then interiors filled with as long strokes as possible. Sharp corners, the serifs of letters, the tips of leaves, hairs and claws, for example, are accomplished by lifting the brush as it moves from the inside of the shape, towards the outside. For very square corners, the tip of the bristles may be laid on from the inside of the shape.

169

For the finest of lines good eyesight and featherlight control is needed. The last two or three hairs only are used, in a vertical grip, with a delicacy that would be used to drag a vertical needle over the skin without damaging it. Freely flowing paint is needed, with an averagely full brush with the surplus scraped off against the palette edge, and the finest point formed.

For drawing straight lines with a brush, it may be rested against a ruler held at an angle against the finger tips, and rigidly braced.

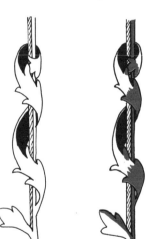

For the blending of gouache colours in flower petals, in twists of ribbon and medieval styles of capitals & borders, the whole area is first painted in white or very light colour. The darkest areas are painted, then a washed and nearly squeezed dry brush pulled through the boundaries. This is repeated until the desired degree of blending is achieved.

170

Outlines and highlights are added last.

For good flower painting one has to look at the living plant, at least making a sketch and colour notes. A wet in wet watercolour technique is a good starting point for a modelled underpainting. This can be followed by fine watercolour or gouache detailing.

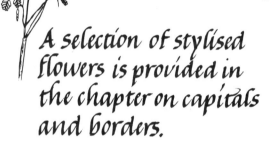

A selection of stylised flowers is provided in the chapter on capitals and borders.

HERALDRY

The design of heraldic devices is a subject in itself. Though there is some variation possible in designs of the mantling (originally a cloth over the helmet as protection from the sun), or the compartment or ground on which a shield might stand, the heraldic description of a coat of arms must be adhered to. The structure of the crown is important and a study of armour will give added awareness for accurately proportioned details of helm and shield. Different ranks require different helm designs. The number of twists in the wreath is important, and books on such subjects must be consulted before making one's own designs.

The colours used tend to be vivid. Small gold details will probably look best in shell gold or even gold ink. Silver (Argent) is usually left white – though aluminium or platinum leaf can be used.

It must always remain obvious that red is really red & cannot be confused with purple, hence Vermillion or Scarlet Lake is a good choice.

Yellow can be used instead of gold, but it should be a gold tone.

Cobalt Blue is appropriate.

The green used must be halfway between yellow and blue with no hint of either hue.

14··Using·Gold·
·and·Other·Metals·

There is something very special about opening a book,
turning the pages, and watching different areas
of each page sparkle and light up as the light falls on
different areas of gold. Similarly, to walk past a framed,
illuminated piece of work produces different reflections
at different angles, and it seems to have a life all of its
own.

The use of gold in comparative terms to its effectiveness, and the number of hours involved in a piece of work,
is not expensive. A sheet of gold leaf 10 cm x 10 cm (4″x 4″)
can be purchased quite cheaply. When next to so-called
gold ink, the difference is extremely obvious. Gold ink may
be useful for fine lines or tiny details in heraldry, but it
tarnishes quickly.

The brightness of gold depends on the type of gold used,
how it is attached to the work and whether or not it is
burnished. On one design a mixture of techniques can be
used, to produce some areas with a mirror finish whilst
others have a more matt appearance.

Gold will not stick by itself. Shell gold is powdered gold mixed with gum. It is sold as a miniature brick on a china tile, but originally it was sold on half a mussel shell. A drop or two of water added to the side of the gold enables the particles to be dislodged with a brush & made into a type of ink. Experience will determine the consistency needed for use in a pen for small writing, or for painting over colours as dots or fine lines (taking care not to disturb the paint.

Shell gold was also used for backgrounds in medieval times. If a fine-pointed agate burnisher is available, dots and lines can be burnished with pressure, or areas can be made more reflective with the use of a wider tool. Backgrounds can be laid either before or after the painting has been done. Letters drawn (which is not easy as the particles tend to settle out of suspension) can be polished, too, by gentle & then harder pressure of the burnisher, using it in a circular motion. Every so often, the burnisher is wiped on a silk cloth. If the powder has a tendency to fall off the work, an extra drop of gum arabic solution can be used in the mixing. However, if too much gum is used the surface will later crack.

Transfer gold is the easiest sheet gold to use as it is attached to an oiled paper and cannot blow away. It is supplied in books of 25 sheets — but some firms will sell it by the single leaf. If no other forms of gilding are attempted, all calligraphers should try attaching transfer leaf to gum ammoniacum as it is just about foolproof.

The areas on the manuscript that will be gold have to be completed before colour is added (or the gold may stick to the paint too). The usual order is writing, gilding, then painting.

Gum ammoniacum can be bought ready for use, or prepared as follows —

1. Choose a glass jar that can be thrown away after use. Cover the granules with warm water in the jar. Stir well and leave overnight.

2. Add a small pinch of sugar, a small volume (about $\frac{1}{8}$th of the final volume) of concentrated chloroform water to inhibit mould, and a little red watercolour to just tint it.

3. Place the container in warm water, and restir.

4. Strain the mixture thoroughly through a few thicknesses of nylon stocking material, or an old handkerchief, into storage containers. Do not squeeze the material or grit will come through.

BEWARE! It is a messy, sticky process. Water will wash out some of it when fresh.

Unwanted gum may be removed from dried brushes with acetone – but this is not beneficial for the bristles. It is better to wash brushes immediately after use.

The solution can be used in dip nibs or quills for writing or brushed into drawn areas, or added as spots. Enough has to be laid so that it is obviously shiny when dry. Whilst an area is still wet, more can be added to build up a raised effect. More is needed on paper than on vellum.

When dry it will go clear, usually after about 15 minutes, depending on the degree of raise. The gold leaf can then be added. The gum is breathed on from close range with long deep breaths from deep down in the lungs. Immediately the breathing has been completed (I try about six breaths, each lasting five seconds) the transfer gold is placed over the now sticky gum, and as much pressure as possible applied vertically, with the thumb, over a hard surface, on top of the backing paper. Any twisting or scrubbing may damage the gum surface, which can become too sticky with too much breath. It is best to do small sections at a time, possibly cutting the sheet of gold leaf with scissors into more manageable rectangles.

If the gold has not stuck or is patchy, more can be applied over the top. Usually failure to stick is caused by not enough breath or not enough pressure, but more gum can be painted over the top if all else fails. Surplus gold from around the edge of the shape can be removed with a silk cloth or dry brush – but it can be erased or scraped as a last resort. An ink eraser cut into wedges with a knife is often useful for this purpose.

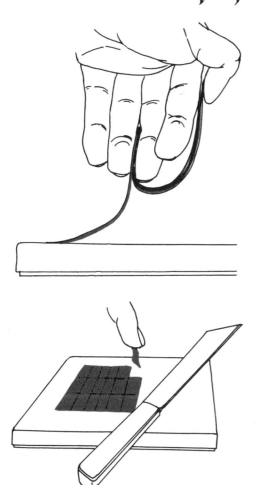

Loose gold leaf can also be applied to gum ammoniacum and is slightly brighter. It is usually handled by opening the book from the back and laying a leaf on a soft gilder's cushion or suede covered pad. This in itself is not easy for the beginner. It is then cut with pressure and a gentle saw action of a grease-free silk polished knife, into convenient sections. Each is picked up in turn on the end of a finger (moistened with a touch of grease from the hair or brow if necessary), laid over the breathed-upon gum, & then pressed firmly into place through a sheet of glassine paper.

The brightest gold results from burnishing loose gold, laid on a raised hard gesso. This is not easy at any time, but particularly for the beginner. There is no better treatise on the technique than that described by Donald Jackson in 'The Calligrapher's Handbook' (Taplinger, 1986). It is hoped that the following account will enable the adventurous to make progress.

The gesso or raising preparation contains Armenian bole (or jeweller's rouge), coffee sugar, Seccotine fish glue, powdered white lead (lead carbonate) and slaked dental grade of plaster of Paris. The slaked plaster is produced by adding 500 grams of the finest plaster of Paris slowly to a plastic bucket of water and stirring for one hour. The next day the water is decanted, the bucket refilled, and the plaster re-suspended and stirred for ten minutes. This latter process is is repeated daily for a week, then on alternate days for the next month. The plaster is then squeezed dry in a cloth that will not shed fibres, moulded into small bricks, and left in a dust free place to dry. It can then be wrapped and stored.

To make the gesso the plaster must be scraped freshly from a block. Proportions worked out by Irene Base and other workers are by volume (perhaps measured out by the leveled saltspoon)~

16 parts slaked plaster ; 6 parts white lead ; 2 parts crushed crude coffee sugar ; 1 part glue

Although a mortar and pestle can be used, most prefer a ground glass slab and a glass muller for the next stage.

178

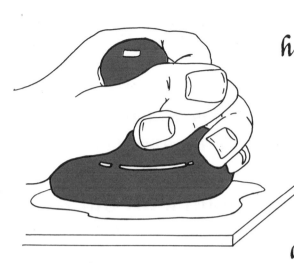

The dry constituents are heaped into the centre of the plate and the glue and a few drops of distilled water added to a central 'crater'. A pinch of bole is added &, using a spatula, a paste is formed. The grinding process will probably take about 45 minutes. Small amounts of the mixture can be ground separately until there is no possibility of large grains being present. These can be transferred to the edge of the plate with a spatula, then recombined and reground. Extra water can be added but the mixture should remain a fraction thinner than toothpaste, so that it just moves as the plate is tilted.

The gesso is transferred to silicon release paper (as used in baking) or aluminium foil, and left in about 5cm (2in) diameter discs. Just before they are dry they are marked into eight segments and left. They may be covered by an empty box, to dry in a dust free atmosphere for a day or two.

To use the gesso a segment (which should contain the ingredients in the correct proportion, as the glue tends to settle around the edge) is broken into small chips in an egg cup. Either distilled water or glair (see painting chapter) can be added. Glair gives a brighter result, but it is harder to attach the gold. You can gild sooner with glair. Glair can also be mixed with water. Add only about two or three drops at the start and leave them for about 15 minutes to be absorbed. The aim is to make the chips into a paste with no enclosed air bubbles. A matchstick or glass rod can be used to push the particles together, then stir in a little more water or glair — about seven or eight drops, perhaps. The creamy liquid can then be used with a pen or moist brush and left to dry. Air bubbles in the mixture may be removed with a needle, or touched with a needle moistened with clove oil. This latter remedy is the last resort.

Occasional stirring of the mixture is necessary to keep the constituents evenly distributed. The work is obviously best kept horizontal for the laying down of the gesso. The application of gold should not be attempted for two or three days if water has been used, or at least six hours for glair. However, the work can be left much longer. Surface unevenness can be lightly scraped with a surgical blade.

The best days for laying the gold are not the best for burnishing. A humid day enables the gesso to remain sticky longer after breathing on it, giving more time for gold application. Final burnishing can be done later in a dry atmosphere. Some people prefer to direct their breath through a tube of bamboo or blotting paper. The loose gold leaf should be on the finger tip beside the breathing tube, the burnisher at the ready, and a silk pad held in the other hand to press the gold on to the gesso the instant the moistening has ceased. Burnishing takes place with great sensitivity, and a circular rubbing motion. At first only the weight of the burnisher is used, then the pressure built up gradually. Layers of gold can be built up on top of each other.

Some people prefer to push the gold on to the gesso through glassine paper (crystal parchment) and burnish over the paper before directly burnishing on top of the gold. The edges of shapes can have the gold pushed on to them by drawing over the paper with a very hard pencil. Experimentation will soon develop an individual approach. Burnishers must be polished with silk often.

If the day is too humid, the gesso remains soft on the surface, and burnishing will tear the gold. About 65-70% humidity seems about the best compromise.

Gilded letters to be left in isolation are usually left unoutlined, as can many decorations. Some features, such as centres of flowers and dots, can sparkle more, however, if placed with colour around them and leaves, for example, may similarly have a line drawn around them. These ideas and many more are expanded upon in the chapter on Decorative Capitals and Borders.

Silver leaf tarnishes in the atmosphere, so aluminium or platinum leaf are used instead. Platinum leaf is hard to obtain, and aluminium is thick and hard to use for the beginner. Aluminium leaf is best applied to gum ammon iacum only.

15 · Decorative · Capitals · · and · Borders ·

It is surprising how little added colour is necessary to bring to life a page of writing or even a small saying. Painted capitals do not always have to be surrounded by intricate patterns, and the use of gold is not a prerequisite — though it can add a magical sparkle and light up a page, and should be used by all calligraphers for some work. Different styles of writing and texts benefit from different treatment. Any decoration should enhance the text rather than dominate or swamp it, and balance it in weight and colour. However, a large decorative capital, may be with complex borders, can be considered a work of art in its own right & framed accordingly.

With regular patterns on single sheets it is probably easiest to trace over single units either on a light box or with the master taped to a window. A photocopy of the final version is also worth keeping for future use, for spacing, the design, or both.

Sometimes it is helpful to design two of the corners first, and develop the border from these, dividing the space evenly if required, and determining the position of other corner devices. The corners should be a little stronger than the borders themselves. If repeating units do not fit evenly around the border they can start separately from each corner and a flower or other appropriate decorative device drawn in the centre space created.

The writing of a text is usually completed first, and then decoration and borders added. After gilding, all areas in one colour are completed, and then all areas of the next colour and so on until the work is finished.

If the piece is large it is a good idea to cover over much of it with a separate sheet of paper, so that the hand does not smudge or damage earlier work, or rub sweat into the surface.

Most capitals drawn are versions of Roman or Versal

letters. A study of these earlier chapters, and practice in drawing the letters should be attempted first.

The examples should act as a stimulus for personal development, and are the merest tip of the iceberg of historic and modern possibilities.

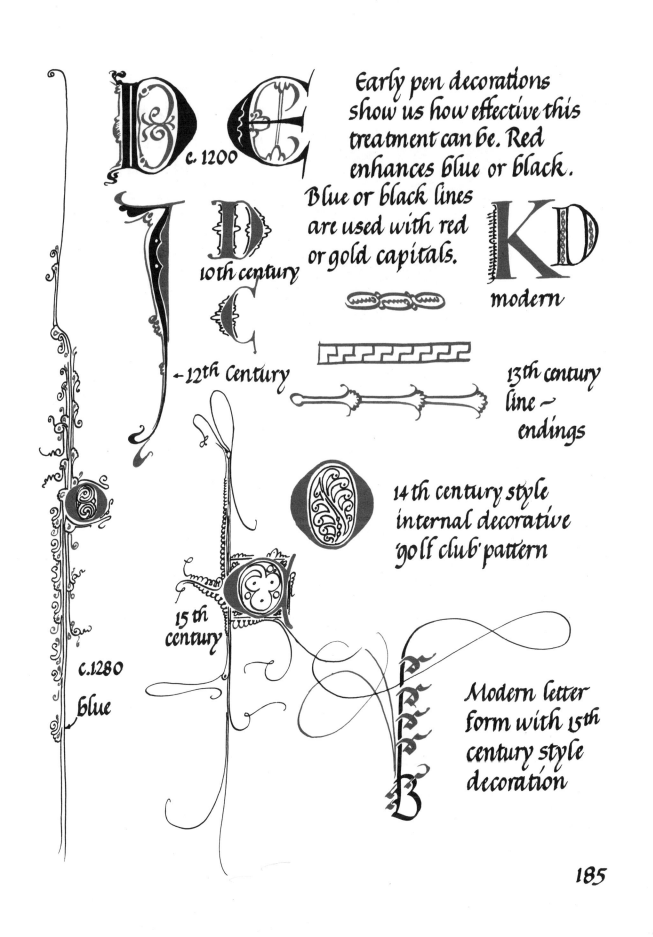

c. 1200

Early pen decorations show us how effective this treatment can be. Red enhances blue or black. Blue or black lines are used with red or gold capitals.

modern

10th century

←12th Century

13th century line ~ endings

14th century style internal decorative 'golf club' pattern

15th century

c.1280 blue

Modern letter form with 15th century style decoration

185

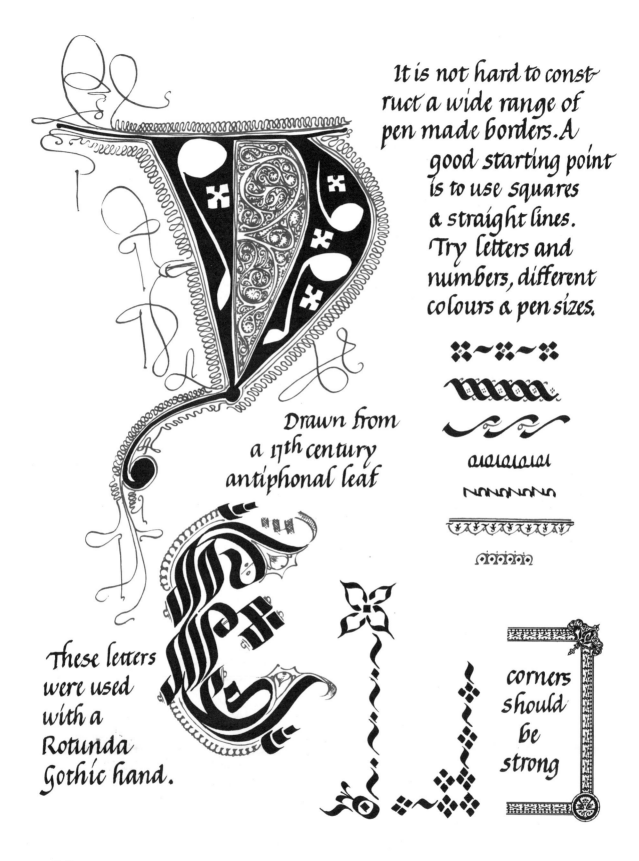

It is not hard to const-
ruct a wide range of
pen made borders. A
good starting point
is to use squares
a straight lines.
Try letters and
numbers, different
colours a pen sizes.

Drawn from
a 17th century
antiphonal leaf

These letters
were used
with a
Rotunda
Gothic hand.

corners
should
be
strong

Pen made 'borders' may be used to outline letters, inside hollow versals or over paint or gold (which will need an application of gum sandarac), as line endings, between verses and as tail pieces, or mixed with painted or gilded borders.

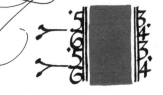

Different letters and numbers can be used on each side.

A simple and appropriate border for Celtic styles consists of red dots.

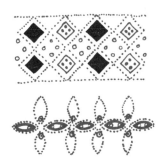

Colour used in capitals does not touch the letter.

THESE BLACK LINES SHOW AREAS OF COLOUR NOT OUTLINES)

No part of the Book of Kells was gilded. Colours used included yellow, vermillion, pale and dark blue, browns, crimson, green, all shades, between pink and purple, but study of colour photographs is necessary to appreciate the subtleties of the hues.

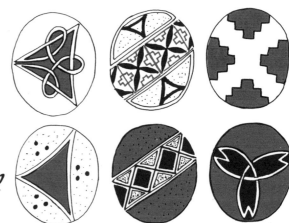

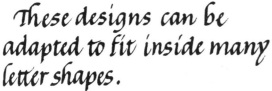

These designs can be adapted to fit inside many letter shapes.

It is too hard for us to draw many of the minute complex knot and spiral patterns used originally. Details of methods that can be used for larger versions are given by George Bain in Celtic Art=The Methods of Construction, Constable 1981. A panelled border is an alternative, some with solid colour inside, others with simple knots or geometric designs. Animal features may be included in the border or drawn outside it.

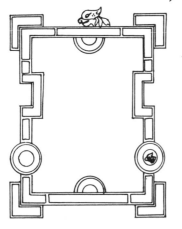

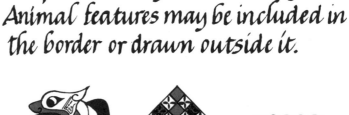

Gold may be used for borders or capitals

All knots, single or as a border, are constructed by drawing either side of a pencil line, alternating over and under crossovers, then removing the guideline. There are many knot patterns. This one is particularly useful as the ends close easily.

An effective construction for capitals is a hollow letter formed from a gold outline. A thin black line touches the inside of the gold, and a thick black line touches the outside. Red dots border the entire letter, and any knots and spirals that may be added to the ends of the limbs.

one of many variants of key pattern

The inside space between the gold can be filled with knots or other designs, or solid colour, for example bright blue or crimson, without touching the rest of the letter.

Titles can form a border when written in straight line letters. Colours may be varied between letters, and decorative devices or panels used between words and in the corners.

As shown, dots may be used as an alternative.

189

The design of miniature paintings inside letters is beyond the scope of this book. However, the chapter on painting techniques should assist in experiments in copying or adapting medieval styles.

Carolingian and Foundational Hand capitals should not be heavily exaggerated as versal letters, but stay much closer to Roman monumental letters in proportion than do Gothic initials. They may be executed in paint, or gilded, with any decoration selected in weight to suit the script.

All plant borders and additions, whether realistic or stylised, whatever the writing style, are constructed according to the following principles—

1. They start from a definite point.

2. Main stem lines curve ⟨ or ⟩, and probably many side branches too.

3. In nature leaves grow from the stem forming a V pointing towards the root. The bud will produce a new branch, leaf or flower—

or

NEVER

flower—

Branches get thinner towards the tips.

Leaves should be

TRY GOLD CENTRES
IN FLOWERS

OPPOSITE
or
ALTERNATE

Italic and light weight Roman styles often look best with fine Roman capitals, gilded perhaps, & delicate plant borders.

 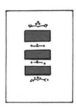 

These border designs suit any style.

This form of decoration is called white vine work. Simple examples were developed in the

- ▨ Gold
- ▨ Emerad Green
- ☐ Natural paper or vellum
- ■ Prussian Blue
- ■ Flame Red (watery?)

eleventh and twelfth centuries from carol-ingian capitals like the one drawn below, the finest being drawn in Italy at the end of the fifteenth century. Borders can similarly

191

be constructed. They go well with Carolingian, Foundational and Humanistic hands, especially when written small.

Another Renaissance Humanistic technique was to enclose a painted capital in a box painted with a shell gold background, and a shell gold background used in the border with naturalistically painted flowers and insects.

Gold capitals were also used with shell gold lines drawn on a painted background. Gold ink may be used for this purpose.

The white lines could be shell gold

The letters were often given a three dimensional appearance, as was the border to the box.

The construction of boxes around letters was featured in most Gothic manuscripts, the Luttrell Psalter being an ex~ ception~

After the Luttrell Psalter c. 1335- 1340. Gilded E (though similar initials could be painted in gouache) Watercolour background

■ Ultramarine blue with a touch of white or Cerulean blue
□ gold   ⇒ white lines

Though other borders were often added, the edges of the letter protrude through the first box.

The colour and the gold meet. The gold is laid first, then the paint (dense gouache in the main), next a black outline to everything (gold, letter, stem and leaves), and lastly white lines added.

Though Gothic styles are not favoured by many for general use, borders and patterns can be adapted for modern work, and capitals may be framed or used, possibly, for bookmarks.

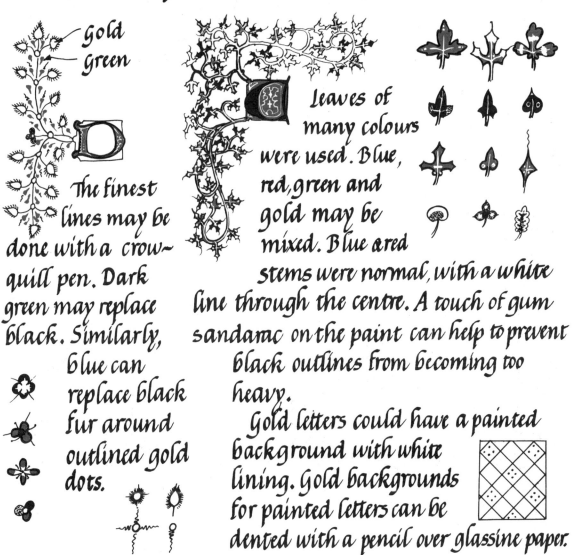

Gold
Green

The finest lines may be done with a crow-quill pen. Dark green may replace black. Similarly, blue can replace black fur around outlined gold dots.

Leaves of many colours were used. Blue, red, green and gold may be mixed. Blue a red stems were normal, with a white line through the centre. A touch of gum sandarac on the paint can help to prevent black outlines from becoming too heavy.

Gold letters could have a painted background with white lining. Gold backgrounds for painted letters can be dented with a pencil over glassine paper.

193

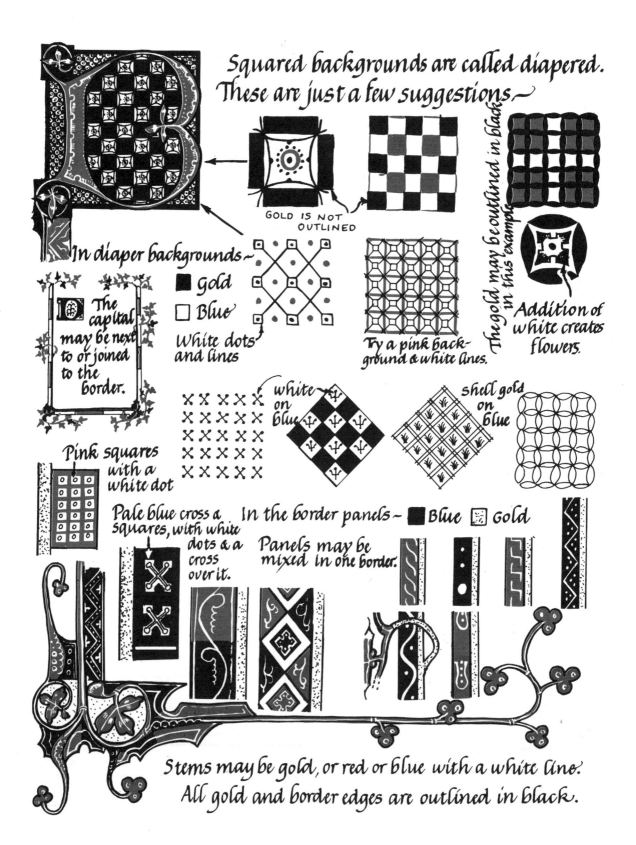

Squared backgrounds are called diapered.
These are just a few suggestions~

GOLD IS NOT OUTLINED

The gold may be outlined in black in this example

Addition of white creates flowers.

In diaper backgrounds~

■ Gold
□ Blue

White dots and lines

Try a pink background & white lines.

The capital may be next to or joined to the border.

white on blue

shell gold on blue

Pink squares with a white dot

Pale blue cross & squares, with white dots & a cross over it.

In the border panels~ ■ Blue ▣ Gold

Panels may be mixed in one border.

Stems may be gold, or red or blue with a white line.
All gold and border edges are outlined in black.

194

capitals may have leafy trails which are entwined around a gold and coloured stem, and dry brush colour-blended as described in the painting chapter.

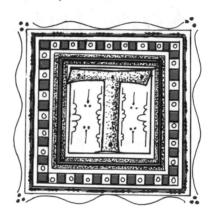

Border patterns and decorative devices can be combined to make an interesting and precious looking illuminated letter. Experiment!

In this example — 1. Gild a letter 2. Paint a blue background 3. Leave a small space 4. Two parallel gold lines with red in between them 5. Leave a small space 6. Alternate blue and red squares 7. A paler blue spot in each blue square 8. Leave a small space 9. Touching red and blue lines with small white decorations along the boundary 10. Outline the letter and all boxes and borders with black 11. Add a fine pen border.

Letters can be used to make patterned squares in a border.

Small white leaves are effective on colour next to gold, or on the boundary between red and

GOLD

blue lines drawn to touch each other.

16·Making·Your·Own·Pen·— ·Stick·Ink·Preparing·Vellum·—

Cutting a pen for oneself enables control to be exerted over the flexibility and width of the nib, the sharpness, the pen angle (to suit your writing position & the style being written), and ink flow. Over thousands of years, scribes have used reeds for pen construction, for their flexibility, lightness and responsiveness. Experiments should be made by harvesting older stems at the end of the growing season, storing indoors for a year or two, & then cutting as described. There are a few stockists of suitable supplies. Bamboo is an enjoyable alternative, but has a heavier feel than a reed.

A length of hollow reed or bamboo cane is cut off, about 1 cm (½ in) wide, and 15 cm (6 in) long. Often the best cane pens come from lengths that have been stored indoors for over a year, like reeds.

With a stiff straight edged blade, e.g. a Stanley knife, initial cuts are made to leave a nib of one thickness of cane wall.

Carefully scrape a flat surface –
this will contact the paper and must
be hard, with all traces of pith removed.
   By cutting a parallel flat surface on the
top of this nib greater spring will be
created.
   The sides may be trimmed, parallel,
to the nib width desired.

   A razor blade can
be very carefully slid along the
centre of the nib, with the grain.
This helps the ink to flow.
   The most important part is pre-
paring the writing edge. On a very hard
surface – metal, stone, hard plastic or glass –
a shallow cut at about
30 degrees, then another
at about 60 degrees, can
be made with a very
sharp, stiff, straight blade.
   To make sure the edge is true, a check should
be made with a magnifying glass. The shallower the
angle of cut at the tip, the finer will be the thin lines
produced, but the nib will need recutting more often.
   Before use, the nib is soaked in ink for a while to help the
flow. When writing, the nib can be dipped into ink.

197

Wiping the top edge with an old well-washed cotton cloth, piece of suede, or sponge helps to prevent blobs, and it will soon be discovered how much ink is needed and can be loaded without drips. Preloading with ink, which can also be done with a brush, for each letter can be expected if the nib is broad.

Reservoirs for ink are useful, particularly for wide-nibbed pens, and can be fitted to touch either the top or lower surface of the nib, leaving a square of reed or cane at the tip. Strips of plastic from cream and yoghurt cartons may be used, particularly those with a curved base.

rubber tube

Metal reservoirs can be cut and bent from clock springs that have been de tempered by heating red hot and cooling slowly. Strips can be cut from drinks and other tins, but great care must be taken with the sharp edges.

Reed and bamboo pens have a particularly good feel to them on paper. In their preparation, many techniques are used that are the same as those required for cutting quills.

Quills, when properly cut, and used with the best ink,

are like reeds in that they have a feel to them that proclaims that they really are the best tool for the job, particularly on vellum (though they also write superbly on paper). They are not easy to prepare, and some experience in writing is probably necessary to appreciate their capabilities and the fine details of their preparation. They are almost weightless, can fit the hand perfectly, and can produce the finest of lines and the most fluid of writing and flourishes. My knowledge of their preparation has been gained through one of Donald Jackson's workshops and my own experience since, and I gratefully acknowledge his advice and instruction.

Substantial swan, goose, or turkey wing feathers that have been moulted are the best, and the barbs should be cut off without damaging the barrel and the length reduced.

Quills are selected to fit the hand well — usually those from the left wing for right handed people. The end is cut off, and the feathers stood in water overnight. To harden them, all the water is shaken out and the inside membrane carefully removed. A pan of hot silver sand, or paver grouting sand, is prepared on a stove, or in an electric frypan. A personal temperature preference will be developed. One where drops of water will evaporate almost instantly is a good starting point.

 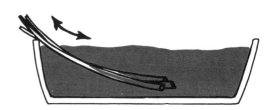

The quills are filled with the hot sand with a spoon, & then the shafts submerged rapidly by pushing them into the pan of sand, waiting two or three seconds, and removing them. This is repeated until they turn from milky to clear with a tinge of brown.

If the sand is too hot they will bubble and burn, or be too brittle. If it is too cool, they will stay soft. If only the tips burn, the rest of the barrel may be cured satisfactorily. The outside membrane of turkey quills bubbles, but below this should remain smooth.

The sand is shaken from the feathers immediately they harden, and the outside flakes of membrane are polished off with a rough fabric, or scraped with something blunt. At this stage they are still slightly soft and can be pressed and held against a hard surface to flatten them slightly, if a wider nib is needed.

200

To cut the nib, a quill knife is required. Those bought usually have to be resharpened on a carborundum stone to produce a blade with a cross-section as shown, gently curved on one surface, flat on the other and stropped on leather to razor sharpness.

Much practice and experimentation is needed to get the feel necessary to control the slit splitting, even cutting of shoulders and fine trimming.

The slit is put in first by raising the knife blade in the barrel. After a small start is made, the slit can be elongated by jerking a paintbrush handle in the same way as the knife is used. The slit is supposed to stop where the thumb nail is held over the top, and should be in the centre of the quill when held comfortably in the writing position.

Cuts are made from the back, about 3 cm (1¼ in) from the end of the slit to cut away about half of the barrel.

By twisting the quill, and the wrist holding

←3 cm→
(1¼ in

the knife, the knife blade is maintained at right angles to the barrel wall as the side cuts are made to form the nib shape

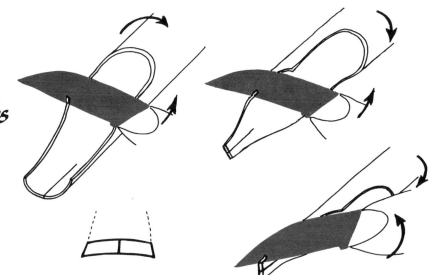

and width. A slightly longer period of sharpness results from the slightly tapered cross-section. These cuts start just behind the termination of the slit. When the tip is trimmed, the slit will be about 1½ times as long as the width of the nib desired, but can be longer if the pen is to be used for gesso for gilding.

If the nib width is such that only the edges of the tip touch the writing surface, due to the circular nature of the barrel, the underside will need to be flattened by taking off fine shavings of material.

remove

The final writing edge is cut as for reed and bamboo pens, with two cuts. A third cut removing only a tiny wafer may be necessary for a perfect edge. The angle of the writing edge to the axis

of the barrel is selected according to the pen angle needed
for the script being written, and the most comfortable
writing position.

A reservoir
can be fitted,
and with a
sloped board
the quill may be tilted above
or towards the horizontal to
help control ink flow.

arrows show the
position of the end of the slit

The nib may be retrimmed by
the finest shavings being removed
from the underside of the point, or from the front edge
(being careful not to change the nib width), perhaps two or
three times before a recut is needed.

Having prepared a personalised
pen, an ink that flows out at the ideal
speed for one's own writing has to be
obtained for the best results. Chinese
stick ink, rubbed on an inkstone with
a few drops of distilled water, can
produce a perfect consistency & density,
and can be loaded with a brush.

from the underside.

Well prepared vellum is a joy to write on with most pens,
but particularly with a quill. Vellum can be made from

calf, goat or kangaroo skin, and small and large pieces can be obtained from several stockists. For preference, writing is done on the hair side only. Untreated, it is an ideal medium for painting and illuminations and is well worth the small extra expense involved. However, for writing areas, it should be prepared at least by sandpapering thoroughly with 320 grit 'wet and dry' abrasive paper, then 400 grit, to raise a very slight velvety nap to the surface, without roughening it. The rubbing of pumice powder over the skin prior to sanding can help remove grease. After dusting the surface and ruling lines, finely ground gum sandarac, contained in a closely woven cloth bag is dabbed on the writing area, rubbed gently, and every scrap of dust removed. The vellum is then ready to write on.

The colour variations of vellum, its texture, and longevity help to make it an exceptional writing surface that should be tried by all serious calligraphers. For those who become users of large areas, or who wish to use it for the pages of books, study of Sam Somerville's chapter in 'The Calligrapher's Handbook' (Taplinger, 1986), would be worthwhile. Problems arise in stretching and these he discusses fully, but for most framed jobs of average size, this is unnecessary. However, prior flattening of a sheet is possible to a large extent by relaxing it in a humid atmosphere, then placing a fairly heavy board over the top. If a work in progress is to be done in several stages covering and weighing down may be necessary in between work sessions, as sheets may curl if left. However, due to differences in thickness and structure of the skin near the spine and down the sides, different areas stretch at different rates in any change of humidity. A slight ripple in the surface of a large sheet is therefore always expected.

Any stretching and mounting on board is done after writing has been accomplished, so a small pad of paper can be used under the skin for a softer writing surface. It should be expected that pens used on paper will not have the same feel on vellum and changes will probably have to be made to the ink flow rate for maximum effectiveness. A well cut quill, beautifully prepared vellum, and ink of just the right consistency can add a new and exciting precision and dimension to writing.

17·· Further · Reading ·

ANGEL Marie · Painting for Calligraphers · Pelham
    Books · London · 1984 ·

BACKHOUSE Janet · The Illuminated Manuscript ·
    Phaidon · Oxford · 1979 ·

BAIN George · Celtic Art ~ The Methods of construction ·
    Constable · London · 1977 ·

BICKHAM George · The Universal Penman · Dover · New
    York·1954 ·

BROWN Peter · The Book of Kells · Thames and Hudson·
    London ·1980 ·

CHILD Heather Ed. · The Calligrapher's Handbook ·
    Taplinger · New York · 1985 ·

GOURDIE Tom · Calligraphic Styles · Studio Vista ·
    London · 1979 ·

GRAY Nicolete · Lettering as Drawing · Taplinger · New
    York·1982 ·

JACKSON Donald · The Story of Writing · Studio Vista
    London · 1981 ·

JOHNSTON Edward · Writing and Illuminating and

Lettering · John Hogg · 1906 · Pitman · 1948 ·
Now published by A and C Black ·

KNIGHT Stan · Historical Scripts : a handbook for
calligraphers · A and C Black · 1984 ·

LEHMANN-HAUPT Hellmut Ed. · The Gottingen
Model Book · University of Missouri Press ·
Columbia · 1978 ·

MARKS Richard and MORGAN Nigel · The Golden
Age of English Manuscript Painting 1200~
1500 · Chatto and Windus · London · 1981 ·

WELLINGTON Irene · The Irene Wellington Copy Book ·
Pitman · London · 1977 ·

·Acknowledgements·

I would like to thank all those who lent me historic scripts and work for the colour plates. Work of Ethna Gallagher, Barbara Nichol and Margo Snape is reproduced by permission of The Pen Shoppe Collection.

My thanks are further due to Rob Heyman Photography for photographing the work Kate Beukes, Jon Case, Douglas Eising, Ethna Gallagher, Don Hatcher, Barbara Nichol, Margot Snape, Vi Wilson, and my own.

I am also grateful to Pat Rowley for permission to use the bifolium from a proof in the development of her book 'The Ark and Mrs Goose', and R. Mudie for permission to use Ian Mudie's poem 'This Land'.

The books listed for further reading are those I have found especially useful, and acknowledgement is made to their authors.